Clam Gardens

Published by New Star Books

Series Editor: Terry Glavin

Other books in the Transmontanus series

1 A GHOST IN THE WATER   *Terry Glavin*

2 CHIWID   *Sage Birchwater*

3 THE GREEN SHADOW   *Andrew Struthers*

4 ALL POSSIBLE WORLDS   *Justine Brown*

5 HIGH SLACK   *Judith Williams*

6 RED LAREDO BOOTS   *Theresa Kishkan*

7 A VOICE GREAT WITHIN US   *Charles Lillard with Terry Glavin*

8 GUILTY OF EVERYTHING   *John Armstrong*

9 KOKANEE: THE REDFISH AND THE KOOTENAY BIOREGION   *Don Gayton*

10 THE CEDAR SURF   *Grant Shilling*

11 DYNAMITE STORIES   *Judith Williams*

12 THE OLD RED SHIRT   *Yvonne Mearns Klan*

13 MARIA MAHOI OF THE ISLANDS   *Jean Barman*

14 BASKING SHARKS   *Scott Wallace and Brian Gisborne*

16 WRECK BEACH   *Carellin Brooks*

17 STRANGER WYCOTT'S PLACE   *John Schreiber*

Clam Gardens

ABORIGINAL MARICULTURE
ON CANADA'S WEST COAST

Judith Williams

TRANSMONTANUS | **NEW STAR BOOKS** VANCOUVER

Butter and littleneck clams, cockles, and a horse clam.

Head-Wolf and those who had him for their Chief lived at Ebb-Tide-Beach south of Crooked-Beach. Born-to-be-the-Sun [Mink] lived at Crooked-Beach. The people of Head-Wolf were always happy because they had many kinds of shellfish to eat, for the tide always went down to their beach. The tide did not go down on Crooked-Beach, and those who lived at Crooked-Beach were always hungry. Born-to-be-the-Sun always felt badly. He lay on his back in the house to think what to do.

When night came, Born-to-be-the-Sun made himself small. He stole Head-Wolf's son from his house and returned to Crooked-Beach. When Head-Wolf discovered his child was gone, he got into his canoe with his speaker and came to Crooked-Beach searching for the boy. Born-to-be-the-Sun's mother, Had a'wa, went out of her house. She called to Head-Wolf to make the tide go down to the shellfish and his son would be returned.

Wolf's speaker called: "Bring the child and the tide shall go down to the barnacles."

Born-to-be-the-Sun's mother asked: "What good are these barnacles?"

The old man spoke again: "It shall go down to the seaweed."

"Of what use is seaweed to us?"

Then Head-Wolf's speaker spoke again: "Bring the son of our Chief. The sea shall dry up everywhere."

"That is too much," Born-to-be-the-Sun's mother said. "You have done too much! Why is it not enough to wish that it may go down to the rolling stones?"

The speaker called: "Bring the son of our Chief. The ebb tide will not pass the rolling stones."

Thus Born-to-be-the-Sun obtained the tides of our sea. Now all the myth people were rich, for they ate clams and all kinds of shellfish.

FROM A TLAWITSIS STORY IN
Kwakiutl Texts BY FRANZ BOAS
AND GEORGE HUNT, VOL. 10 OF
The Jesup North Pacific Expedition

for Keekus

*A Broughton
Archipelago
clam garden.*
PHOTO BY DR
JOHN HARPER
AND MARY
MORRIS

CONTENTS

Prologue		9
1.	Keekus	15
2.	Raven Walk	21
3.	Best Clams On the Coast	31
4.	Open That Envelope, Please!	43
5.	Who, When, Where, and Why?	53
6.	Other Directions	63
7.	Abode of Supernatural Beings	82
8.	Gathering at the End of the Road	91
9.	'We Can't Count the Years ...'	100
Epilogue		113
APPENDIX *Clam Bake*		120
ACKNOWLEDGMENTS AND SOURCES		123
INDEX		126

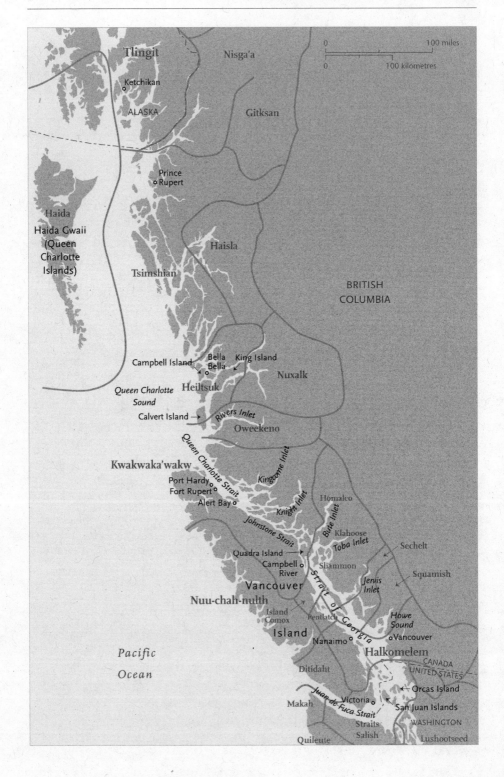

Tlingit

Nisga'a

Ketchikan

ALASKA

Gitksan

Haida

Haida Gwaii
(Queen
Charlotte
Islands)

Prince
Rupert

Haisla

Tsimshian

BRITISH
COLUMBIA

Campbell Island

Bella
Bella

King Island

Nuxalk

Heiltsuk

Queen Charlotte
Sound

Calvert Island →

Rivers Inlet

Oweekeno

Kwakwaka'wakw

Queen Charlotte Strait

Kingcome Inlet

Port Hardy
Fort Rupert

Alert Bay

Knight Inlet

Homalco

Bute Inlet

Klahoose

Toba Inlet

Sechelt

Johnstone Strait

Quadra Island →

Campbell
River

Sliammon

Jervis
Inlet

Squamish

Vancouver

Nuu-chah-nulth

Strait of Georgia

Island
Comox

Penlatch

Howe
Sound

Vancouver

Island

Nanaimo

Halkomelem

Pacific

Ocean

Ditidaht

CANADA
UNITED STATES

Juan de Fuca Strait

Makah

Victoria

Orcas Island

San Juan Islands

Quileute

Straits
Salish

WASHINGTON

Lushootseed

0   100 miles

0   100 kilometres

PROLOGUE

On my long map of the northwest coast of North America, coloured pins notate a sequence of indigenous clam garden locations that begins at Orcas Island in the American San Juan Islands. The pins extend up to Quadra Island, north to the Kwakwaka'wakw islands west of the mouths of Knight and Kingcome inlets, skip to Heiltsuk territory around Bella Bella, and end near Sitka, Alaska, where Dr. John Harper saw clam gardens from a helicopter in 2005. Red dots pinpoint clam gardens I've investigated, yellow indicate those located by Dr. Harper from the air, and white dots mark sites identified by Native people, like K'uk'agunolis (meaning "stone walls put up at the side of a beach"), which is behind a small islet north of Port Neville in Johnstone Strait.

FACING PAGE: *Vancouver Island and the northwest coast of North America, with distribution of Native territories.*

This map evolved from correspondences noted between explorers' descriptions, Native stories, features of land, and piles of stones — not newly stacked, not natural — whose revealed purposefulness cracked open a track to the past that overturns accepted concepts of Native food systems and economics. It's an exciting route.

Everyone asks "What is a clam garden?" Fisherman, logger and upcoast raconteur Billy Proctor built his own Broughton Archipelago clam garden over a forty-year period. Native people taught him that a clam garden "was a clam beach that was tended with great care and a lot of work. Rocks were gathered up from the sandy beach area and piled in a ring along the low-tide perimeter. The removal of the rocks made more room for the clams, and the wall of stones prevented the sandy beach from eroding."[1]

I became fascinated by these remarkable structures in 1993 after I was sent to see clam garden structures on Quadra Island by Klahoose elder Elizabeth Harry (Keekus). That visit led me to the proposition that those clam gardens, and similar structures that I began to add to my map, were created when indigenous people, seeking to maximize clam production for an expanding population, rolled boulders to the extreme sea edge of a butter-clam-bearing location to create a ridge parallel to the shore. Doing this extended the depth of beach out from the shore, and by integrating a series of small beds, it sometimes greatly lengthened the width of the butter-clam-bearing substrate.

Ongoing rock moving during succeeding harvests raised and levelled a larger portion of the naturally sloping beach, and since butter clams grow only at the very lowest levels to which the tide drops, a larger area was available more often and allowed for longer harvest periods. Over time the cultured strand came to be composed mainly of clam shell fragments and the biogenetic sand resulting from shell decomposition. The major bivalve fostered by this energetic cultivation was *Saxidomus gigantea*, known as the butter clam.

A parallel investigation began in 1995 when marine geomorphologist Dr. John Harper was mapping British Columbia coastal areas from a helicopter for the provincial government. John saw many kilometres of what he thought must be human-made rock walls. Like all scientists, he was trained to prove truth from hypothesis, via observation and experimentation, to fact. However, it seemed that the hypothesis he developed about what he was convinced were human-made walls and terraces flanking the Broughton islands could not be proved through available marine geographic theory, and it was unacceptable to British Columbia archeologists who, quite remarkably, seemed to know nothing of the walls' and terraces' existence. The rock structures John had seen were so numerous, and the territory they covered so extensive, that experimentation seemed unwieldy, and his penultimate move was to locate an informative Native source. That route ran smack up against a Sasquatch carrying away four bags of clams. It's unnerving when it becomes clear your authentic source believes in what you are trained to consider fable. You can dismiss your source or you can change. John decided to accept traditional Native knowl-

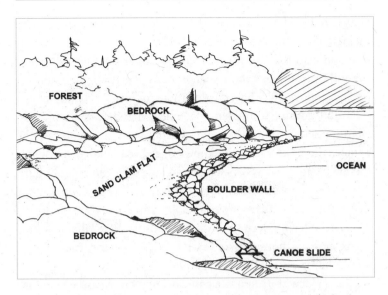

FOREST

BEDROCK

SAND CLAM FLAT

OCEAN

BOULDER WALL

BEDROCK

CANOE SLIDE

Clam garden.

edge as validation for his conviction that Native people had not only dug natural clam habitat, but, in favourable locations around the Broughton islands, had erected a complex of rock-walled terraces that suggest what we call mariculture.

Bringing these Native mariculture structures to light may be termed, by some, a "discovery," although the clam gardens, as will be shown, were never lost. Given the evidence of Native knowledge and usage that has also come to light, it's prudent to sidestep that term. Let's just say that the story of the re-emergence of these rock structures makes visible to the non-Native world a mindset-altering number of boulder walls, which were erected by Northwest Coast indigenous people at the lowest level of the tide to foster butter clam production. The number of gardens, their long usage, and the labour involved in rock wall construction indicate that individual and clustered clam gardens were one of the foundation blocks of Native economy for specific coastal peoples.

As in all good stories, acutely differing angles of observation add a certain tension to the tale. This one circles warily around the perplexing absence of textual reference to these major food-gathering sites in both biological and archeological reports, and the bemusing indifference of contemporary archeologists to my initial report of the gardens' existence, as well as to Harper's science-backed efforts to gain their attention. Far from just noting the location of rock terraces built to grow clams, the story of the disclosure of the clam gardens' existence inevitably wanders into the ineluctable connection between land forms, food, territorial control, and claims about rights, ownership, gender authorship, and the authority to speak about such matters. It places a high value on the local knowledge that revealed them for my consideration.

Possibly nothing would have become generally known about the clam terraces without the right questions being asked of Native people who hold traditional knowledge about, and currently use, the foreshore. Keekus's answer to my 1993 question regarding traditional Klahoose food sources led to the startling consideration that indigenous systems of sustainable clam production on the BC coast preceded modern shellfish mariculture installations by hundreds, perhaps thousands, of years. It fuelled watery expeditions to an escalating number of clam gardens.

This is a new story and rife with speculation. New data emerges sporadically from both Native and non-Native sources. However, if the clam gardens, as observed and recorded by the initial cast of acute observers, are accepted as an essential *cultivated* unit of Native economy, a term like "hunter gatherer," which has been used by social scientists to define Northwest Coast Native society, must be reassessed. The convenient conviction that explorers and settlers were entering unowned virgin wilderness will evaporate like fog.

For me there is also a deeply affecting aesthetic and an ecological lesson in the stretches of carefully constructed rock walls in Waiatt Bay, around and over which swirl the tides of the clam garden story. Need was so harmoniously mated there to site, and a solution to the problem of increasing food supplies so elegantly resolved, that the rock-walled terraces were assumed to be natural formations.

In Tsikya'les ("with big clams"), there lived a chief who had a daughter and a big dog. The chief found his daughter had lain with the dog, who he killed. He extinguished all fires and abandoned his daughter, but the girl's grandmother had hidden a glowing coal in a shell so the girl was able to light a fire. She soon gave birth to ten puppies and, in order to feed them, lit fires on the beach at night to search for shellfish. Down on the sand at night she heard the puppies in the house singing "Tsi'kyala Iaia — look for shellfish mother." One night she crept home to find the dogs had taken off their skins and danced as people. The mother threw most of the skins in the fire, and the dogs who were unable to regain their skins remained human.[2]

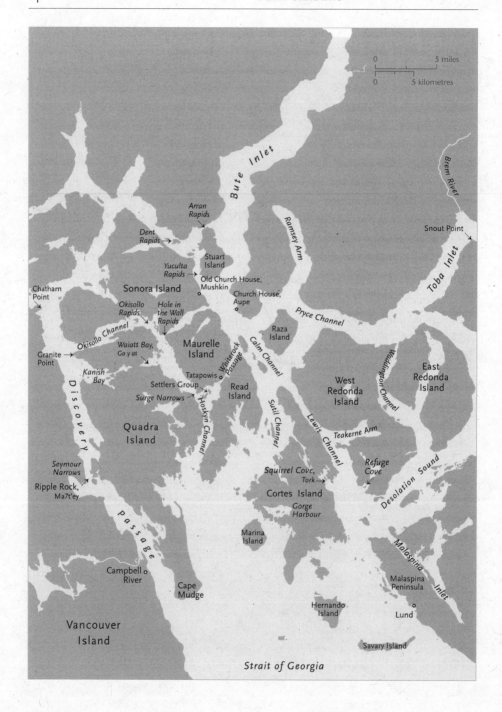

0   5 miles

0   5 kilometres

Bute Inlet

Brem River

Arran
Rapids

Ramsey Arm

Snout Point

Dent
Rapids

Toba Inlet

Stuart
Island

Yuculta
Rapids

Old Church House,
Mushkin

Chatham
Point

Sonora Island

Church House,
Aupe

Pryce Channel

Okisollo
Rapids

Hole in
the Wall
Rapids

Raza
Island

Okisollo Channel

Granite
Point

Waiatt Bay,
Ga y at

Maurelle
Island

Calm Channel

Weddington Channel

East
Redonda
Island

Discovery

Kanish
Bay

Whiterock
Passage

Tatapowis

West
Redonda
Island

Settlers Group

Read
Island

Surge Narrows

Hoskyn Channel

Sutil Channel

Teakerne Arm

Lewis Channel

Quadra
Island

Refuge
Cove

Desolation Sound

Seymour
Narrows

Squirrel Cove,
Tork

Ripple Rock,
Ma7t'ey

Cortes Island

Gorge
Harbour

Malaspina Inlet

Passage

Marina
Island

Malaspina
Peninsula

Campbell
River

Cape
Mudge

Lund

Hernando
Island

Vancouver
Island

Savary Island

Strait of Georgia

1

Keekus

In January 2004, a fat brown envelope arrived on my desk at Refuge Cove in Desolation Sound, 160 kilometres north of Vancouver. Inside, clipped to a mass of reports, newspaper articles, and aerial photographs, was a letter from Dr. John Harper describing his sighting of an astounding number of rock-walled "clam gardens" and his efforts to establish that they were human-made. Terry Glavin, who'd profiled this work in the *Georgia Straight*, had suggested John extend his current researches to me since I was thought to "know about clam gardens." Indeed I did. However, in the eleven years since a Klahoose tribeswoman had told me of clam terraces in Waiatt Bay, I'd found only one other non-Native person who understood their use and significance. Here, remarkably, was John writing that he'd spent seven years trying to prove to himself, and a resistant Government of British Columbia Archeology staff, that over 350 Native-built clam gardens had been constructed on the foreshore of the islands of the Broughton Archipelago on the mid-coast of British Columbia.

FACING PAGE: *Waiatt Bay (Ga y at), Kanish Bay, Quadra Island, and surrounding territory.*

The mass of papers slipped from my hand and I laughed and laughed! John certainly had my sympathy.

In 1993, I'd been preparing the visual art installation *High Slack* for the UBC Museum of Anthropology (MOA).[1] The work circled around an 1860s conflict between Chilcotin people and a road crew building Alfred Waddington's toll road from Homalco territory in Bute Inlet to the mainland interior gold fields. My search for the name of the Klahoose (Tl'uhus) Chief who thrice rescued road surveyor Robert Homfray from death in 1862 led to Klahoose genealogist Elizabeth Harry at Sliammon Village near Powell River. The Klahoose/Homalco/Sliammon grouping — the Mainland Comox people — are now the most northern speakers of the Mainland Comox dialect of Salish. Elizabeth, known as Keekus, her sister, Susan Pielle (Thapwuut), and brother, Chief Joseph Mitchell (Heowken), had been traditionally raised by their par-

ents, Rose and Chief William Mitchell, and Rose had been an important source of history and food gathering and preserving techniques for the book *Sliammon Life, Sliammon Lands.*[2]

Genealogy is a great Native pastime, and one sunny day, as we lay on the grass watching a Sliammon soccer tournament, Keekus and Susan engaged in lively calculation as to who was related to who and when. Keekus's proposal that Homfray's saviour might be Kla-

Elizabeth Harry (Keekus) greeting canoes at Sliammon Village, 1989.

PHOTO
COURTESY
MICHELLE
WASHINGTON

hoose Chief Yay K Wum rounded out the surveyor's description of this resourceful man. I learned then the importance, as the story of the clam gardens demonstrates, of searching for First Nations oral history to confirm, augment, or correct assumptions about Native land use, ownership, or historical interaction.

Later, as we checked details for *High Slack*, Keekus suggested I take our boat north through the rapids to Quadra Island and look at rock walls her people had long ago erected around Waiatt Bay. The walls, well known to her grandparents, were built, she said, to raise the level of clam benches that could only be harvested at the lowest tides of the year. In the terraces created by the walls grew the butter clams that had been a staple unit in the Native diet. Her family still harvested the Waiatt clams, which they considered the best on the coast, and she said they repaired the walls when needed. She warned me to go at a zero tide.

On an August morning, a day offering the last real summer low tide of that year, I set out in our speedboat, *Tetacus*, with my friend, artist Corrine Corry. The tide began its drop to a noon low of 0.8 metres as I followed Keekus's directions to Waiatt. I headed up Lewis Channel, crossed Calm Channel, and planned to push through Whiterock Passage and Surge Narrow rapids at slack water. I'd never done such a thing by myself — a fact I did not mention to my companion — although we had recently boated as far as Tatapowis, the abandoned village on the north side of the pass.

If you consult marine chart #353901, as I was doing, you'll note that the bay to which Keekus directed me lies at the heart of a group of islands whose narrow connecting channels are marked with numerous current arrows. Rocks are rather freely scattered in inconvenient places. The *Coast Pilot* notes tides at the entrances to these channels can run twelve knots at the flood and ten knots at the ebb. With Corrine's help, I lined up the markers that allow passage west through Whiterock Passage at low water, with the daunting field of boulders fronting Tatapowis rising safely starboard and not through the boat's bottom. We cruised north up through the Surge at a flat slack, although the *Coast Pilot* warns of a one-metre wall of water at the flood of an extreme tide, and, of course, an extreme low tide is needed to see the walls. I tied to a kelp bulb off Antonio Point to further study the chart. The *Coast Pilot* notes that the south entrance to Waiatt Bay is "encumbered" by rocky protuberances, and that feature, as well as the shallow and narrow north entrance, is, I think, as important to what I subsequently found there as the dominant cool flow south through the Okisollo Channel rapids.

Once we were inside arrowhead-shaped Waiatt Bay, the sea was glassy calm. Keekus's directions had been a trifle sketchy, so I proceeded to a likely looking bay, directly ahead, on the north arm of the bay. I butted *Tac*'s bow against a ledge to catch my bearings.

Tetacus *at Terrace Bay clam garden, Waiatt Bay, 1993.*

Waiatt Bay terrace with exposed wall and central stone.

The water, near level with the top of the ledge, dropped conveniently away, and the boat floated above clear sand two metres below so a grounded engine was unlikely to disgrace my seamanship. We disembarked, tied *Tac* to a boulder, and realized we'd come ashore against a remarkable, inward-inclining boulder wall of considerable length. Exploration to our right and left indicated the wall sinuously wound around the bay, following its contours. The depth of what I felt should be called a bench, or terrace, from the compact boulder wall to rocky shore, varied from 2.5 metres at its southwestern end, where it seemed to have been built out from a steepish cliff, to approximately 4.5 metres where we'd come ashore. It then swooped into the centre of the small bay, deepened past a tidal island, and headed along the opposite side to a slightly southeastern point.

As we strolled the spouting, oozing, sucking terrace, it seemed a live thing, as if, in construction, the builders were able to enhance the life of an existing locus — not by replanting every year, but, as the West Coast Natives did when digging clover roots in the deltas of the long inlets, by reburying new growth into a habitat enhanced through the repeated cultivation resulting from harvesting. "Making things better for the next time, removing stones," as my old friend Walter Franke said he did when digging clams. This, I assume, is the bedrock of all husbandry; enhancing what is there, increasing its density and size, but working with what wanted to grow, what the terrain suggested or insisted. The walls were the elegant evidence of — what? Hundreds of years of enhancement?

I was standing on an ancient living entity that could be destroyed in minutes by thoughtless bulldozing.

The water was clear, but the rising tide caused the undulating kelp growing out of the front of the wall to obscure its actual form, so I swam along its length to assess its height. At the outer, southwestern edge, the wall seemed all of 2 to 2.5 metres high. It declined in height as it ran into mid bay, where it was easy to scramble up rocks piled less than two-thirds of a metre high. A canoe could easily slide ashore there onto soft mud. The wall increased in height again as it swung out on the other, less groomed, side of the bay. Outside the wall, the submerged bottom of the baylet was unbroken white sand. A walk up to the mid-bay trees revealed a low overpass north into a bay central to Octopus Islands Provincial Marine Park.

Way too soon the tide rose across the bench and I had to wade to undo my rock anchor. We took *Tac* to the southeast arm of Waiatt Bay and swam around in the warm water over a wide mud flat. It didn't appear built up, but once the tide rose, the walls seemed almost a hallucination.

Suddenly Corrine stood up and said, "Look!" The water surface was repeatedly pulsing a good twenty centimetres up and down her body, yet the water in the bay itself appeared to remain still. Suddenly it dawned on me that this fascinating sensation indicated the tide had changed to the flood; the sea must be pouring rapidly into the narrow north entrance, perhaps being sucked out the southern one. I drove *Tac* south through the well-named Surge Narrows on water a surprising ten degrees off horizontal. It was, however, going our way.

Next day I reported my findings to Keekus. "Oh no," she said, "you didn't see it all — it's *all* around the big bay. You need a zero tide."

I was left with a considerable number of questions and called the Archeology Branch of the BC Heritage Conservation Department to report the rock walls and seek enlightenment. Not a bit of it. They were insistent that (a) they had recently surveyed Waiatt Bay — they had the site reports to prove it — and no

Homalco village of Church House in 1994. The church was built in 1896.

such walls had been found, (b) there was nothing in the literature
to indicate indigenous mollusc mariculture, and (c) if indigenous
rock construction existed, it was a salmon trap. Keekus's information was discounted.

I was puzzled. My husband, Bobo Fraser, called his soccer
buddy Calvin Harry, whose family had lived at New Church
House, which was, in recent times, the closest occupied Native
village to Waiatt from the mainland side.

"Waiatt? Oh yeah!" Calvin said. "That's where we go for
clams."

2

Raven Walk

It was not until the next June, when the tidal cycle entered its lowest range for several days, that Bobo and I were able to head north. When we entered Waiatt Bay, the wall I'd previously seen was exposed a good forty centimetres above the surface of the sea. Bobo, our pals, sculptors Susan Schelle and Mark Gomes, and I each took a slow careful walk along the entire length of the terrace. The walls' inward-canted, serpentine embrace of the cliff reaffirmed my initial impression that their carefully engineered forms were as elegant as equally pragmatically generated Mayan highways in the Yucatan. Near the narrow southwest end, I was berated by a quartet of ravens in black tie and tails whose luncheon I'd interrupted. Stray needle fish, dismembered crabs, vermilion stars, contracted fluorescent anemones, open lolling cockles, sea lettuce, whelks, and clams were set out as if at a seaside diner. I retreated and sat on a boulder, and the ravens, bold as brass and twice as arrogant, snacked their way down the beach towards me. Deciding I was a harmless nuisance, and definitely unwilling to give up his soon-to-be submerged feast, one hopped on a rock thirty centimetres away, cast a repressive eye in my direction, and sorted crabs from the bladderwrack with a thick sharp beak. The cocky critters only halted their truffling when one found a large and especially desirable gift from the undertow. The others would engage in a curious stiff-legged hop, bumpf! bumpf! bumpf!, sideways towards the tidbit possessor. A discussion would ensue. While they were distracted, a mink scrambled down, fossicked in the rock wall, and ran his find up the beach.

Tidbits consumed, the ravens continued to belly on down the clam bed, their huge gleaming blue/black tails slicing back and forth over the shell strand. One expected them to light up post-prandial cigars.

As I returned to my boat, the ravens ascended into trees and began cleaning their beaks on bark. I found my companions spreading local goat cheese on sourdough bread and munching imported black Greek olives. A swift bidding war commenced for the coffee in my thermos. High bid was a bag of chips. A hot cup of coffee in the wilderness, like a stranded flounder on the terraces, has a distinct value.

You might wonder, however, why we were not eating butter clams from the benches. Well, the bureaucracy has decreed this bay, in summer, is a veritable soup of PSP, the paralytic shellfish poisoning popularly known as red tide, which butters and mussels retain longer than other molluscs. Signs with red crosses through clam images are nailed to trees.

The first note of red tide poisoning occurs in Captain George Vancouver's *Journals* when a crewman became ill from eating mussels at Poison Cove in Mussel Inlet off Mathieson Channel. The toxin derives from poisonous planktonic dinoflagellates on which bivalves feed. Although harmless to molluscs, it can be fatal to humans. In BC, the dominant toxin form is saxitoxin (SXT), derived from the microscopic one-celled organism *Gonyaulax catenella* or *Gonyaulax acatenella*. PSP may colour water red, although not all red blooms are poisonous. Symptoms of PSP poisoning include numbness in the lips, tongue, and extremities and a final loss of control. The only known treatment involves doses of an emetic and a rapid laxative. Don't touch those butter clams!

The problem is that signs are put up and seldom removed since there is insufficient funding for regular testing of the actual poisonous state of clams in remote areas. If you consult the Department of Fisheries and Oceans' Openings and Closures toll-free line during summer months, you will find many coastal areas closed to butter and horse clam harvesting, although it is unlikely these areas are being tested at that time. The closures mean butter clams are now seldom harvested by boaters. However, fatalities still occur. On June 7, 1997, a Native resident of Karluk on Kodiak

Port Progress — Pre-emptor with clams and grouse, 1917. "When the tide is out, the table is set. A good week's meat supply. Giant clams. Grouse." BC ARCHIVES #HP078776

Island in Alaska ate six or eight raw butter clams and within two hours had numb lips. Despite purging himself with water, he was dead on arrival at Kodiak hospital.

Questioned later about potential poisoning, Calvin Harry scoffed, "You white guys have no culinary sense of adventure." However, it seems that most Native people knew to harvest butters in winter months, when cold water curtails the deadly bloom, and to remove the gills and siphons, which retain red tide. I had not yet knowingly eaten a butter clam, although I knew early home-steaders considered butters an important dietary item. Author June Cameron, whose family homesteaded on Cortes Island, describes canning with her mother, as most old-timers did, the "wonderfully rich tasting Butter clams" dug in Von Donop Inlet.[1] "Isn't it interesting," she told me, "we never thought of red tide. I don't recall anyone getting ill."

Before this day's tide inundated the evidence, we circumnav-igated the bay and found a considerable number of benches at spots providing an opportunity to build. The rock walls, as Keekus

had said, were built all around the larger bay and round into the
smaller northern loop within the marine park. At the western
head of the bay, a large mud flat extended out from low land where
dense shell midden dripped from exposed tree roots. I followed a
short path over a narrow neck of land into Small Inlet, an inner
loop of Kanish Bay on Quadra's west side. A swim there confirmed
the soupy water slicked shallowly over soft mud a long way out.
Archeological site reports indicated extensive midden in Kanish,
and a large village site. The journey from Kanish to Waiatt Bay
was a simple stroll.

By the time I returned to Waiatt, the tide had slipped over the
benches, anemones unrolled tentacles towards unwary prey, kelp
fronds stretched out in the increasing current, and the enigmatic
walls had disappeared. Time to go.

Bobo finds the atmosphere of rapids intoxicating, and proposed
heading home through Hole in the Wall rapids between Sonora
and Maurelle islands before slack water in order to introduce our
companions to the invigorating game of Okisollo Roulette. He
cruised out the north entrance of Waiatt and slid the boat across
boils the size of houses. At the entrance to Hole in the Wall, water
sloped in varying directions, not all of them going our way.

"Look at that whirlpool!" Bobo crowed.

I was less enthusiastic. I'd heard my pal Arabella Campbell's
story of a trip she and another fishing guide had undertaken south
from Big Bay. Precisely as they got to Hole in the Wall narrows and
a whirlpool opened down, they ran out of gas. The heaviest part of
the boat, the engine, was sucked down into the descending cone,
and they whirled around, ass down, long enough for Bella, who
confidently guided clients through the Arran, Dent, and Yucla-
taw rapids to prized salmon holes, to formulate a troubling new
thought: "I'm gonna die!" Not so. A boat appeared, threw them a
line and pulled them free.

As we were about to hit those narrows, a large plastic cruiser
forced its way through against the flood and chopped the rapids to
bits. *Tac*, apparently seized in the jaws of a particularly bad-tem-
pered rottweiler, was twisted, turned, and banged up and down
at the same time. We took a cubic metre of water over the bow
into what is, fortunately, a self-bailing area and, more alarmingly,
many litres over the stern.

Bobo stopped *Tac* in calm waters to enjoy our expressions, and Mark was delighted. Then he discovered his hiking boots full of water in the bow. Bobo bragged about the shallow draft of his boat. He pointed out his calmness in moments of others' panic, and swept away any criticism of his judgment.

As we flipped coins for the last cup of coffee, I considered what effect the vigorous Hole in the Wall, Surge Narrows, and Okisollo rapids surrounding Waiatt Bay might have had on the choice of that location for such extensive clam production. Nutrients flowed by with considerable velocity, but the bay itself was almost lagoon-like, and the water within was warmer than that in most of the surrounding area. Mucky Owen Bay, east on Sonora Island and opposite Waiatt, was more open to cold northern currents flouncing down Okisollo Rapids and over Gypsy Shoal, and would be less nurturing. The rapids meant unwanted and uninformed visitors could find themselves at the mercy of what can, at the flood and ebb tides, be standing walls of water or the massive boils and downward siphoning whirlpools we had experienced.

I had taken many photos at Waiatt that day to make clear to me and, I assumed, others that the walls were human-made structures. My sharp-eyed companions confirmed that although they might have no other purpose than to raise the level of the clam beds and extend their range and productivity, there was an elegance of engineering to the walls that both pleased the eye and suggested organized industry.

I called the Archeology Branch. Once more I was told that what I'd seen must be salmon traps. It didn't make sense. The mouths of the small Waiatt creeks, where fish traps might logically have been built, were precisely where neither I nor the archeologist who'd undertaken the Waiatt site investigation had found the walled, levelled-to-the-shore terraces Keekus insisted were for clam production.

Several fish-trap forms were constructed in the Pacific Northwest. One is said to consist of a semicircular stone barrier bellied seaward at approximately half-tide level near a salmon stream. At high tide, salmon flowed in over the wall; as the tide ebbed, the stone wall prevented some fish from returning to sea. Another form used two stone lines in a river to funnel fish toward a basket fish trap held between the two arms. Nancy A. Greene has mapped

Salmon weir on the Cowichan River, c. 186–
BC ARCHIVES
#H-06525

remains of very large stake enclosures in Comox Harbour. A chevron-winged form was dated between 220 YBP and 230 YBP.[2]

The Cowichan River photo shows a post-contact weir made of a crib of poles driven into the bottom of a stream or river. The crib opening faced inland, and fence weirs extending to shore funnelled salmon into the trap. Native fishermen used dip nets, deployed off cantilevered platforms, on stronger-flowing rivers like the Fraser and Skeena. Some fish traps were built where currents caused fish to congregate awaiting the freshwater runoff that stimulated spawning. There is a half-tide-level rock circle at the south end of Quadra in conjunction with a fine Seawolf petroglyph, where five species of salmon were known to pass.

Anthropologist Franz Boas records the use of broken-open clams in flounder traps, and both Native history and artifact expert Hilary Stewart and marine biologist Rick Harbo, in his excellent *Shells and Shellfish of the Pacific Northwest*, suggest a possible relationship between fish traps and the walls. Harbo notes that "some coastal aboriginal groups used the white shells of these [butter clam] species in salmon traps, because a layer of white shell on the river bottom enabled fishers to see and spear their quarry more easily."[3]

After my second trip I reviewed my data. What I had seen, in Waiatt territory, was evidence of nearby Native village sites (consumers and labourers), a bay that was a seafood buffet, and some very dynamic water movement that briskly siphoned nutrients into the bay. Fish traps I had seen elsewhere were not in the same position as the walls, nor were the traps filled as the walls were. I had found what social scientists like to call "Native informants" who used the clam gardens, and I could find no reason to doubt Keekus's veracity. However, my off-topic qualifications as artist and UBC Assistant Professor of Fine Arts weren't cutting any ice with the archeologists. Seeking to bolster my position, Bobo and I took onboard Hilary Stewart and anthropologist Joy Inglis, who had worked to have the ancient trail from Waiatt Bay to Small Inlet preserved from logging. We added author Heather and engineer Rolf Kellerhaus, and a geologist, and headed *Tac* to Waiatt at a minimal tide. They seemed open to my proposal that the bay was filled with purpose-built, human-made structures containing clams.

Emboldened, on August 20, 1997, I wrote the archeologists of the Heritage Conservation Department in Victoria to explain what I'd heard and seen, propose the significance of the rock walls, and warn of damage being inflicted by logging. I offered to guide an archeological visit.

There was no reply. Ever.

Busy with other projects, I temporarily shelved plans for publication. The clam benches were still used by local folk, and I'd enjoyed those ravens bellying down the lunch table. I left them to it. But I continued to visit Waiatt Bay, fascinated that these living artifacts had forever erased any lingering notion I might have had that Northwest Coast people had been simple "hunter gather-

Terrace Bay clam bed and logging slash.

ers." What appeared to be mariculture did not seem to fit with the
newer labels for them as "complex hunter gatherers" or the offen-
sive "wealthy scavengers."[4]

From the research I then began for *Two Wolves at the Dawn of
Time*, a history of some Kingcome Inlet pictographs,[5] I learned the
Kingcome River delta, conveniently thought to be open meadows
when settlers pre-empted the land in 1893, had, according to eth-
nobotanists, periodically been burned by the Tsawatainuk to keep
it open and free of unwanted plants. Alan Halliday, the last home-
steader, told me that after he removed his cattle in the late 1980s,
alder steadily encroached into the fields. Ancient sets of gardens
had existed on that wide delta, marked with flags indicating family ownership, and I persistently heard stories from the Tsawatainuk that their wild crabapple "orchards" on the flats had been cut
by settlers, and their clover and silverweed root gardens disrupted
by imported cows and pigs.

Billy Proctor at his museum on Gilford Island, 2005. PHOTO BY IRIS FIELD

The inhabitants of the most complex Native culture in North
America did not wander aimlessly around in the rain hoping to
trip over food. They planned to spend much
of the wet winter indoors, around a warm fire,
with enough dried salmon and smoked shellfish hanging from the rafters, and enough
stored oolichan oil to allow them to invite
friends and rivals around for a bit of dancing
and challenging appetizers of smoked protein
and silverweed roots dripped in grease. It was
perplexing to think that many theories about
West Coast Native culture had been formu-
lated by observers who had taken little note of
Native husbandry and who were, apparently,
unaware of the clam gardens that produced
one of the dietary staples.

In the summer of 2003 we docked our old
seiner, *Adriatic Sea*, at Echo Bay on Gilford Island in the Broughton Archipelago. The tide book indicated there would be fairly
low water the next day, so we took *Tac* around into the neck of
Shoal Harbour in the morning to study a rock-walled structure I'd
noted two years earlier. Although not as elegantly engineered, the
terrace resembled those I had seen on Quadra.

We tied up behind the *Ocean Dawn* at the nearby dock of the *genius loci*, who'd provided me with keys to many upcoast puzzles. Billy Proctor strolled down the ramp from the museum he'd built to house his enormous collection of Native artifacts, antique chainsaws, old bottles, early fishing lures, and what was approaching the complete flotsam and jetsam of 5,000 years' occupation of the area.

"Billy, those rock terraces," I gestured back at the wall, "over there — for clams?"

"Yup! Clam gardens. There's lots more around the Broughton. I'm just writing about them in my new book. Native people built them for clams and over there, in the neck, in spring, they hung hemlock boughs on the clam garden walls and herded herring in with boughs hanging down from the canoe sides. It caused the herring to spawn on the boughs on the walls."

It was Billy's understanding, from a life spent amongst the Native people of the Gilford Island area, that clam beds nearest a village belonged to the dominant family, and families of lesser rank had to enhance remoter beds to ensure clam supply. Butter clams grown in the gardens were, he said, either eaten roasted in their shells at the edge of a fire or braided into chains, smoked, and stored. Billy Proctor not only knew what and where the clam terraces were; he'd also built up one of his own over a forty-year period, and it supplied a good deal of his protein.

That September, in *Full Moon, Flood Tide: Bill Proctor's Raincoast*, next to his neighbour Yvonne Maximchuk's drawing of a Broughton clam terrace, I found Billy had laid out the first published description of these unique structures. He concluded:

> There are more clam gardens in this area than anywhere else on the coast. They are easy to locate at low tide. Look for a wall of neatly piled stones fronting a small flat beach and you have found a clam garden. At some clam gardens there is an additional feature — a space left clear of rocks for the landing of canoes.[6]

Mink was living at Crooked-Beach with all the myth people. He would disappear from time to time to Southend. The people at Crooked-Beach did not know about those who lived there at Behind-Neck, the Starfish-Women, who were digging clams at that place. Mink would go and steal the clams of the women, for Starfish were all female.

One time Mink hid until he saw the women who'd been out gathering clams return and anchor their canoe out. Mink swam out but when he put his hand among the clams he was bitten and began to cry. The women went out to look. One asked why he was crying.

Mink lifted his hand, which was bitten by a large clam. A woman at once broke the clam off his hand and said: "Who asked you to take our clams?"

Mink replied, "Oh my dear! I did not take them. I just made a mistake when I put my hand in this basket with clams in it."[7]

"Waiting for the Canoe," by Edward Curtis, c. 1914, shows two women with clam baskets and digging sticks.

3

Best Clams On the Coast

When Keekus sent me to look at the Waiatt Bay walls, she said that the clam beds there produced the best butter clams on the coast. Waiatt had proven to be filled with a multiplicity of rock-walled clam terraces and sea-eroded "kitchen" middens built up from domestic debris. Many indigenous villages sat atop such middens, which could be up to six metres deep. Most were composed of butter clam shells densely packed within fine purplish soil punctuated by larger horse clam shells. A layer of purple hash indicated the residue of a large feed of mussels, and in northern middens, compacted mussel debris lay under the clam shell layers. The sea-side exposed face of a midden, or the walls of archeological trenches dug into old village sites, strongly suggest that butter clams were a significant component of the diet of coastal peoples. And, indeed, Native folk valued the butter clam which produced a larger and tastier amount of meat than native littlenecks. Butter clams could be woven onto ironwood sticks, smoked, dried, strung on cedar strands, stored, and traded. It made sense to build the rock walls, extend butter clam beds, and create more of the productive mid-beach range.

The structures also enhanced production of horse clams, "harvested in the summer, dried, skewered on waxberry stems, and stored for food or trade."[1] Their shells were used as serving containers, as dippers for skimming oolichan oil during processing, and as knives.

Just when the possibility of enhanced clam production began will only be determined by research into the arrival of molluscs

Exposed six-metre shell midden at Kukwapa village site, Fife Sound, Broughton Archipelago, 1989.

on the coast. In "Quest for the Lost Land," BC scientists Renée Hetheringon, J. Vaughn Barrie, Roger MacLeod, and Michael Wilson combine the data from their oceanographic, geographic, paleogeographic and anthropologic research and suggest that by 13,200 YBP the edible clam *Macoma nasuta* had colonized the mud flat in what, due to sea-level rise, is now Hecate Strait east of Haida Gwaii.[2] The scientists note that, soon after, many species of shellfish were so successful that edible shellfish biomass during the late Pleistocene to early Holocene compares favourably with modern levels. However, there was a decline between 10,900 and 10,100 YBP during a cooler period, when sea temperatures reached less than 9 degrees C. By 10,000 YBP rising ocean levels had severed that land bridge.

Archeological digs at Namu, on the mainland east of the northern tip of Vancouver Island, and in the Berry Island midden, just southwest of the Broughton, indicate people in both locations were accessing food resources about 9,000 YBP. However, knowing it may have been possible to gather some clams at such an early date does not answer the question about when butter clam beds were raised and extended by being walled.

Billy's information that the best clam beds near the village were under the control of a leading family, and that the outer gardens belonged to, and were worked by, lesser-ranking families, indicates there was a need to extend existing beds to produce food not oth-

erwise available for an increasing population, but it does not suggest to what degree the wall building enhanced the quality of the
product. Given the work involved at Waiatt, and certainly in the
Broughton, the ubiquity of the walls must reflect confidence that
they produced optimum conditions required for the flourishing of
more and better quality clams.

On your next fish market visit, notice there are Manila or Japanese clams (*Vererupis philippinarum*) and native littlenecks (*Pro-
tothaca staminea*) next to the Pacific blue mussels (*Mytilus edulis*
or the native *Mytilus trossulus*) for sale, but you'll be hard-pressed
to find fresh butter clams to buy. The majority of clams now sold
publicly are Manilas, whose ancestors hitchhiked from Japan with
seed oysters in the 1920s. The Manilas spread so rapidly that by
1941 they were the dominant clam in Departure Bay. They grow a
shorter, more convenient distance down in mud, sand, or gravel,
and higher in the intertidal zone, which makes them easier to harvest although more vulnerable to freezing. The shells close tightly
for transport but open cleanly when steamed. Although they've
spread to the west coast of Vancouver Island, they do not thrive
in cooler northern water. The purple varnish or mahogany clam,
a recent immigrant from Asia, thrives close to the surface and has
begun appearing in restaurants.

Prior to the arrival of these shellfish immigrants, the bivalves
consumed by coastal people were mussels, giant barnacles, littleneck clams, butter clams, horse clams, cockles,
native oysters, the giant geoduck, and presum-
ably the scallops whose shells form the rattle
that accompanies the important Salish Swai-
hwe mask, whose possession confers wealth and
health.

Once, at Squirrel Cove dock, a Klahoose
acquaintance yelled down, "Like butter clams?"

"Sure," I replied.

"Sell you this sack for ten bucks."

"Done." I took the clams home and made chowder.

The gathering of the butter clams I bought was complicated by
the fact they grow buried twenty-five to thirty centimetres below
the surface in the lower third of the tidal zone, although they

can be found as much as ten metres below zero tide levels. Since clams burrow to a depth permitted by the length of their siphon, immature butters are closer to the surface, although lower than native littlenecks.

In *The Clam Fisheries of British Columbia*, marine biologists D.B. Quale and Neil Bourne note that butters can be distinguished from other clams by the external shell surface's prominent concentric striations and deep winter "checks." "Shells are yellow in the young," according to Quale and Bourne, "changing to grey-white with age although the colour is affected by its substrate. The internal surface is white and smooth, but not glossy. There is a strong prominent external hinge ligament and pronounced umbones."[3] The clam body is large, and since the shell gaps slightly at the posterior end, they transport less well than Manilas.

The larger Pacific horse clam or gaper (*Tresus nuttalli* and *T. capax*) grows under similar conditions to more than twenty centimetres in length and lives at the same depth or as far as ninety centimetres below the sand's surface. It also makes a mighty fine chowder if correctly handled.

Both butter and horse clams like a pure sand environment, and although their vertical distribution varies, the greatest concentration occurs between the zero and 0.9-metre tidal level where the maximum tidal range is four and a half metres. In northern areas, where the tidal range exceeds six metres, the upper limit of occurrence is as high as two and a half metres. On exposed shores clams are stunted.

Butter clam parts and shells. Butter clams ingest phytoplankton, augmented by the odd feed of bivalve larvae and detritus, through their siphon, and excrete pseudofeces from the exhalant siphon. They barely feed in the

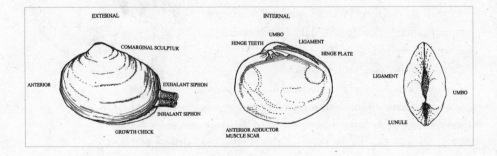

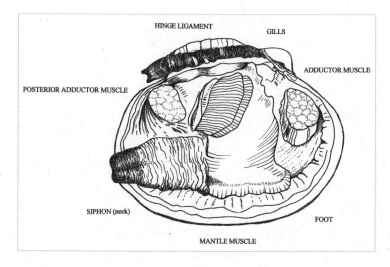

HINGE LIGAMENT

GILLS

ADDUCTOR MUSCLE

POSTERIOR ADDUCTOR MUSCLE

SIPHON (neck)

FOOT

MANTLE MUSCLE

Butter clam interior.

coldest months, which accounts for less red-tide contamination during that period, and they live up to twenty years. Bourne and Quale state that the "greatest concentrations of clams occur where gravel bars are formed by current configurations as at the Seal Islets near Comox."

A significant number of butters are devoured by the moon snail, which lives at similar depths. Using a toothed radula that protrudes from its mouth, this handsome submerged tank drills a hole into a butter clam's shell and over a four-day period consumes the clam.

During our conversation at the Pacific Biological Station in Nanaimo, Neil Bourne explained that while the cockle, found on or near the surface of clam gardens, is hermaphroditic, there are male and female butter clams. Fertilization takes place in surface water, and eggs develop a small swimming mechanism that holds them in place, although currents may carry eggs long distances from parent clams. At the larvae stage the clams resemble specks of black pepper. At twenty-five days they stop floating and, with a newly developed foot, crawl until they attach themselves to a pebble or shell fragment by byssus. They are then referred to as spat. They grow fastest in warm water and at lower levels, although that area also contains more predators. It takes five years for them to grow to the six-centimetre commercial size in the Strait of Georgia — seven years around Alert Bay due to the colder northern waters. There is a distinct advantage to growing clams below Sey-

mour Narrows in enclosed bays that heat up and hold a higher
temperature because they are less affected by the water exchange
caused by tide and current.

Bourne noted that butters like to grow near boulders because
the eddies around them raise water temperature. He said the
Japanese mariculturists sink large cement "boulders," which they
cover with brush in order to increase temperature and spat retention. This echoes the main thrust of an email I received from
Kwakwaka'wakw Tom Sewid, concerning his speculations about
clam garden development.

> Butter clams like to hide around big boulders — we
> clam diggers know this. So after moving some rocks
> [to facilitate beaching canoes], the beach [may] have
> some clams. After working the beach my ancestors
> would have noticed what we call a fluffy beach —
> because of the touch of man. My ancestor says: "We've
> made a productive beach because of working it." It
> would become their property they'd guard with their
> lives because in a still harsh climate, clams could
> mean the difference between life and death.

The notion that building stone walls would enhance clam production could have evolved from observation of the results of inad-
vertent seeding of fish traps or clam growth around the lines of
canoe-slide boulders, which are mainly vertical to the
shore. "Fluffy" is a remarkably evocative description of the biogenetic sand that makes up clam
garden beaches. One might also speculate that
brush laid over clam beaches could encourage
spat retention, as mesh now does in commercial
operations, since it was used to collect herring
roe there.

What might have been less obvious at Waiatt
was the upwelling of nutrients caused by the unique
surging tides. Struck by sunlight and nurtured by heat generated
by eddies around the large boulders situated within the clam flat
and those composing the kelp-draped wall, the nutrients may have
produced more of the algae that feeds sea creatures.

However, Bourne, who had been unaware of clam garden technology, maintained the walls were built to delineate territory and
only accidentally observed to be more productive. He saw ownership as the key to the level of industry exhibited and was dubi-
ous the walls themselves increased nutrients, though they would
gradually increase habitat. He felt that no matter what was done,
it would only raise productivity by 10 percent. This does
not take into account that the large number of beds
in Waiatt would not have occurred without wall-
ing, since much of the shore is steep, and it does
not address the claim that Waiatt clams were of
superior quality. Bourne agreed Waiatt's con-
stricted entrances may have provided longer slack
water, and since clams feed only while under water, the
long high slack of the semi-lagoon conditions may have provided
increased nutrient absorption. He also agreed that the lack of wave
action inside Waiatt would lead to beach stability and retain eggs,
and that the mucky unwalled areas of the bay would smother clam
spat.

What remains perplexing is that no clam researcher, anthropologist, or archeologist appears to have seen or considered important the Waiatt clam terraces or the more than 350 sites Dr. John
Harper calculated he found in the Broughton. Dr. Don Mitchell's
Quadra and Broughton site reports from the 1960s note village
sites, fish traps and rock art, and detail midden dimensions, but
nowhere does he indicate he saw the rock walls or knew of the
clam gardens. Aside from Harper's and my reports, no site report
or book acknowledges them until a cautious note is appended to
archeologist Don Abbot's June 7, 2001, site report.

This silence is interesting given that there existed from the
1920s right into the 1980s an active commercial market for butter
clams. Many Native people were involved in digging, transport-
ing, and processing clams for this market, and as late as 1980, government statistics indicate butter clams were BC's major bivalve
export. Quale and Bourne's 1972 publication clearly indicates
a governmental desire to promote this economy, and they even
report on experiments to remove red tide from harvested butter
clams to increase production. Salmon canneries at Tow Hill in

the Charlottes, Namu, Butedale, and as far south as Redonda Bay attempted to run all year by canning clams in winter when the commercial shellfish harvest occurred.

Butter clams were dug during the two weeks of lows per month from November through January and February, when the tide bottoms out to their level. Economist, author, and fisherman Dr. Don Pepper told me that during the 1940s and 50s, clam digging was so economically important a "Clam Digger's Calendar" was published. Don said that when he dug clams in the 50s, the drill was to approach Dong Chong, the pioneering store owner in Alert Bay, and get fronted $30 worth of bacon, coffee, beans, and eggs. The grub was packed into a sturdy boat alongside buckets, sacks, digging forks, and the essential rain gear. The diggers worked the first available low tide and returned the next night for the next and lower tide, working the beach, or a series of beaches, down to the zero tide and then back up as tides became less extreme. From the Department of Fisheries' Area 12, the northern Johnstone Strait territory that includes the Broughtons, diggers headed back to Alert Bay to sell clams to buyers such as William Scow, who worked for BC Packers.

> *The Olamentko people of Bodega Bay in California say Coyote-man brought the big clam Koo'-tah* (Saxidomus giganteus), *from which pis'-pe the shell money is made, and planted it here in Bodega Bay. This is the place and the only place where the big clam was in the beginning. Wherever else you find it now, the seed came from here.*

Don recalls that Scow packed Broughton-area butter clams on a barge pulled by the seiner *BCP #11* as far south as the Imperial Cannery in Steveston and to Everett, Washington, from the 1930s onward. Scow was succeeded in this enterprise by Harry Shauffer, and in 1960 Don Pepper's partner Byron White transported butters for Clamato. The clam body was sold for ground clam meat, and the liquor became the clam part of Clamato juice. Sometime in the 1970s, I am sorry to report, it was replaced by a synthetic flavour.

In audiotapes made by the Seattle Art Gallery, William Scow proudly announced:

> I'm a clam man. In my job . . . I used to work with a
> biologist when they [wanted] to determine how long

they [clams] would survive with all the digging. "Bill," he says, "the way they're digging they can last for another twenty years, without depleting." I gave all the Indian names for the spots where they dug because there's . . . just crevices here and there. And all those places have Indian names. And I told him . . . the Indians believe . . . There's some high level clams, not right down. When you go clam digging, you think you have [need] a big tide. You don't have to. One half tide. You want a bigger tide, so you can dig longer. But there's some high level clams on the crevices. And I told him Indians believe ducks, when they feed on clams, they drop some on the high level crevices, and so they propagate right there.

The biologist, William added, claimed clams don't move at all, but William said, "You know when you get your clams piled up on the beach; they always fall toward the water. They never fall up; they always fall towards the water. Bags burst and you see them stick their necks out about this long . . . and then they bury in the ground."

William pointed out that his Gwayasdums village was on top of a layer of butter clam shell that went right down to the bed-

Scow fish boat at Gwayas- dums, Gilford Island, c. 1930. PHOTO COURTESY ALVIN SCOW

rock. "Hardly any dirt ... that's all they lived on, was clams. We have the best butter clams on the whole coast [at] Gilford." Scow's claim that they lived on clams makes sense of a taunt, directed from an exclusively salmon-eating member of the Nimpkish tribe to a Gilford boy, that green stuff like that in a clam intestine grew from his belly.[4]

William described clam propagation around Gilford.

> They spawn in the spring of the year ... on top of the soil. And the tide brings them up, and then they drift with the tide, and in three days they grow a shell on one side, and then they drop. And in another three or four days the other side shell grows, and that's where they stay. Some tides ... because the tide is too strong ... the spawn is wasted.[5]

Perhaps scientists and archeologists were never on those dark winter beaches and never saw the distinctive walls at the outer edge of the lowest beds, but what of the biologist William worked with?

Bourne says the market for butters collapsed in 1985. The red tide problem, the loss of markets such as Mott's Clamato Juice, and the public's preference for — and the ease of harvesting — Manilas and littleneck steamer clams combined with the massive spread of popular Pacific oysters to release butters back to Native harvest.

Unfortunately there is a contemporary market for the giant geoduck clam (*Panope abrupta* or *P. generosa*), which is considered a delicacy. The geoduck is found deep in some mud, sand, or gravel clam habitats. Its shell can be nineteen centimetres long, and the siphon, even after it has contracted, will still hang out an impressive twenty centimetres, which gives it a certain erotic cachet in Japan.

A Tlingit mortuary column. The raven sits as a hat on top of his slave, who was to kill the monster clam which lived under a large rock in a channel and pulled down canoes. FROM V.E. GARLAND AND L.A. FOREST, *The Wolf and the Raven*, UNIVERSITY OF WASHINGTON PRESS, SEATTLE, 1948.

At up to four and a half kilograms, it is both the largest and longest-living (146 years) intertidal clam in the world. Mature specimens, at least seventy-five centimetres below a sand surface at the very lowest tide, are difficult to retrieve. My childhood technique, developed on Texada Island, involved a stealthy tiptoe approach across the vast Gilles Bay sand flat so as not to send warning vibrations down through the sand. This was followed by a sudden flinging down of the body and a simultaneous grab at the siphon. A companion then dug down and down around the retreating siphon to the gaping shell as the holder's arm was pulled out of its socket, fingers sank into something weirdly soft, and, prone on the beach, one's armpit was investigated by interested crabs. What then? Since mothers declined to deal with such a creature, we were, fortuitously, seldom successful.

I could now pay a healthy price to eat sashimi geoduck in Vancouver's Japanese restaurants, but the method of commercial harvesting of allowed specimens, which can be seventy years old, is so ecologically alarming I do not. The geoduck, and anything in its immediate environment, is blown loose with compressed air by divers.

However, it is entertaining and perhaps instructive that both Keekus and William Scow claim the clams from the intensively built-up beds in their very different geographical areas are the best on the coast. Did growth conditions and means of production in the Broughton resemble those on Quadra?

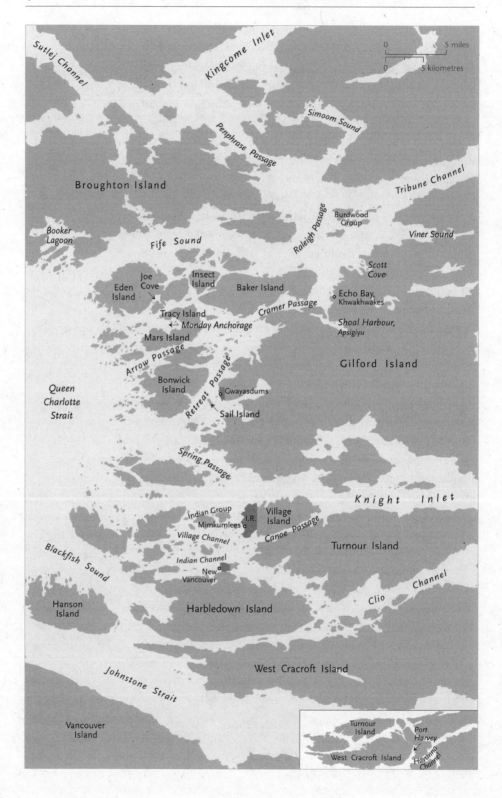

Sutlej Channel

Kingcome Inlet

Simoom Sound

Penphrase Passage

Broughton Island

Tribune Channel

Booker Lagoon

Fife Sound

Raleigh Passage

Burdwood Group

Viner Sound

Joe Cove

Insect Island

Baker Island

Scott Cove

Eden Island

Echo Bay, Khwakhwakes

Cramer Passage

Tracy Island

← Monday Anchorage

Shoal Harbour, Apsigiyu

Mars Island

Arrow Passage

Retreat Passage

Gilford Island

Bonwick Island

Queen Charlotte Strait

Gwayasdums

Sail Island

Spring Passage

Knight   Inlet

Indian Group

Mimkumlees

I.R.

Village Island

Canoe Passage

Village Channel

Turnour Island

Blackfish Sound

Indian Channel

New Vancouver

Clio   Channel

Hanson Island

Harbledown Island

West Cracroft Island

Johnstone Strait

Vancouver Island

0   5 miles

0   5 kilometres

Turnour Island

Port Harvey

West Cracroft Island

Havanna Channel

4

Open That Envelope, Please!

The cornucopia of material sent to me by Dr. John Harper in 2004 contained aerial photographs of clam gardens he'd seen in the Broughton Archipelago, Stephen Hume's *Vancouver Sun* account of John's adventures, and a record of Harper's effort to convince himself, and the Archeology Branch, that Native people had engaged in mariculture by building rock walls that raised the level of clam production to facilitate harvest. John wrote that he'd been told a Native woman, the late Rose Mitchell, had said clam gardens were called *wuxwuthin* in the Island Comox language. John did not know, until we began to exchange information, that Rose was Keekus's mother.[1]

FACING PAGE: *Broughton Archipelago and surrounding territory.*

John had engaged with the clam terrace conundrum from an amusingly antipodean position to mine. On July 15, 1995, working under contract to the government of British Columbia in his role as a specialist in coastal geomorphology, John was 100 metres above a beach in a Bell 206 helicopter, mapping the shore of an island in the Broughton Archipelago, which lies between the mouths of Kingcome and Knight inlets and Queen Charlotte Strait, a hundred kilometres north of Waiatt Bay. Suddenly he thought the foreshore below looked odd.

John's was not an uninformed glance, and his vantage point was unique. Geomorphology is the study of the physical features of the earth's surface and their relation to its geological structures. In order to map the true coastline, Harper and the crew of Coastal and Ocean Resources Inc. had to fly at the lowest point of the lowest daylight tides of the year. If you open your yearly tide book and

Aerial photo of Broughton Archipelago clam garden.
PHOTO BY
DR JOHN
HARPER

check monthly sea-level ranges, you'll not discover many extreme lows during daylight hours. June often contains the lowest daytime tides of the year, although they may not descend every year to a summer zero. It depends. The periodic rise and fall of the sea is due to the attraction of the moon and sun and is affected by the rotation of the earth and our distance from these other bodies at any given time. The tides might descend near or below zero a handful of times in the whole year. That's it. But, as Dr. Pepper had pointed out, descending and ascending tides on either side of a low can be used for harvesting different shellfish species. However, the time of a specific level of tide moves forward daily and is approximately fifty minutes later from one solar day to the next. The year's non-summer lowest tides occur in the dead of the night during the coldest months of the year.

On John's low-tide July day, the curiously uniform foreshore below reminded him of a mapping job he'd done in Labrador, where stone ridges were relics of sea ice pushing against the shore. He wondered if the same kind of ice conditions that had created the ridges in Labrador might have occurred in the Broughtons long ago.

Harper had the helicopter set down on the flat area behind the wall and asked himself just what he was looking at. A curved bay lay between two chunks of bedrock that embraced an extensive, oddly flat beach (known as a berm) with a pronounced rock crest at its outer edge and an abrupt drop-off beyond. The walls appeared to be built of human-portable boulders of uniform size, and the surface within the walls was composed of whitish clamshell hash (biogenic sand), which butter clams prefer as a habitat. What was striking was that this beach was only one of many seemingly organized shorelines he'd seen that day. John flew on to complete the day's mapping, but could not shake the notion that he could and should prove the structures human-made. He thought that might be news. What followed was a diligent application of what he considered the appropriate scientific methodology, which he hoped would lead to a conclusion, acceptable to his peers, that the rock walls were human-made.

With his wife, marine biologist Mary Morris, and James Haggarty of Shoreline Archeological Services, John laid out his initial findings in "Final Report: Broughton Archipelago Clam Terrace Survey" for the Land Use Coordination Office of the BC Ministry of Government Services in 1995. Harper wrote that what he'd seen at one place was a metre-high terrace with "a boulder/cobble ridge in the lower intertidal." He explained that the terrace extended across small embayments or indentations in the mostly rocky shoreline and that above the boulder wall he'd found "a sand flat extending from the ridge into the middle intertidal zone [that was] comprised almost entirely of biogenic sand (giant barnacle and shell fragments)." He reported the area with the greatest density of rock terraces similar in structure to this appeared to be between Broughton and Gilford islands in southeastern Queen Charlotte Strait, precisely where Billy Proctor had indicated to me that there were more clam gardens. The aerial video survey allowed Harper to calculate that the assembly of clam terraces "accounted for over 14 km of shoreline and that 365 clam terraces could be documented." This was an astounding number.

Working with what information he'd been able to gather to date, John concluded his report by stating that the origin of the Broughton ridges was "unknown" (which later would prove not to be so) and that they were not still being actively modified, which, given the butter clam economy of the 1940s to 1980s, described in Chapter 3, cannot entirely be the case. Although that main market for butter clams ended in the mid-1980s, the St. Jean Company still sells canned butter clam meat and nectar on the web and in fish markets, and the backbone of the BC Ferries' clam chowder is butter clams sourced from Mac's Oysters. Both companies acquire butters from the Alert Bay area (Area 12). Representatives of Mac's Oysters state the clams they buy are dug by "Gilford people." Kwiksootainuk people, many of whom still live at Gwayasdums, on Gilford Island at the heart of the Broughton Archipelago, have continued to harvest and to repair their productive butter clam beds because clams remain, for them, an important aspect of their domestic and commercial economies.

Area 12 clams are still attractive for commercial harvesting since they are said to be less contaminated by red tide. This may be the result of the strong influx into the Broughton of cold water, driven west in summer through Queen Charlotte Strait from the gap between the top of Vancouver Island and Calvert Island, combined with the winter's easterly, glacier-iced outflows from Knight Inlet. From late fall to early spring, water temperatures range around 7 to 10 degrees C near the surface and about 7 to 8 degrees C at depth. However, summer temperatures in protected embayments can rise to 15 degrees C.

After Harper's initial sighting and a close study of the 1995 mapping tapes, and despite being unable to find anyone who agreed with his theory, John was convinced the walls were not natural features. But, by his own admission, he seemed unable to prove that was so. He had flown archeologist James Haggarty to the Broughtons and set him down on a clam bench, but the most John could get out of him was that he could not say they were human-made but he could not say they were not. Haggarty added there was nothing in the "literature" about such things. Of course the "literature" referred to was a body of material in Archeology Branch files that was composed of the field notes of professional anthropologists and archeologists and the site reports of professionals and interested amateurs, as well as the body of writings by social scientists about the economic and social structure of the indigenous peoples of the west coast. John could not prove the existence of the Native structures because there was no *written* record that someone had previously said they existed. No one seemed inclined to believe John's trained eye. Interestingly there was a written report in the files containing Keekus's information about Waiatt Bay and my observations there of the clam terraces she had described.

John Harper is a determined and resourceful guy, and when he felt conventional geomorphology could not prove the existence of prehistoric mariculture organized on a thought-provoking scale, he and Mary Morris switched to a study of clam habit and habitat. John confirmed that clams grow in the one-to-three-metre intertidal zone, and the terraces he'd found were all at optimum clam production level. He discovered harvesting improves productivity as long as undersized clams are left covered and no area is cleaned out. Harper looked at clam terraces in relation to Native village sites, which he thought might indicate population densities needing increased clam production. However, in his letter to me, he wrote: "for five years I couldn't find a single person that knew of them or believed they were man made."

Billy Proctor and John Harper. From Ancient Sea Gardens: Mystery of the Pacific Northwest.

Of course, that did not mean there were no folk who knew of clam gardens. It's well to keep in mind that amongst the upcoast clam-digging fraternity, both Native and non-Native, lurks an understandable desire to draw a veil over the location of a productive beach. Getting them to share their site with outsiders is on a par with extracting from a bosom pal the source of the morel mushrooms she just fed you.

John started to read anything on the Broughton area, discovered my *Two Wolves At The Dawn of Time,* and finally came across *Heart of the Raincoast,* Alexandra Morton's biography of Billy Proctor. He quickly realized Billy dug a lot of clams from the Broughton islands and wrote asking his help. In a September 2000 letter, Billy replied that what John had seen were the clam gardens he'd learned about as a child from Native elders Peter Moon, Tom Wamish, and Billie Sandy Willie of Kingcome. Harper's methodology changed. He enlisted the help of Randy Bouchard and Dorothy Kennedy, then working on an annotated translation of the anthropological work of Franz Boas. Ethnobotanist Nancy Turner introduced John to Kwakwalla linguist Daisy Sewid-Smith and to Qualicum Chief Kim Recalma-Clutesi, who is married to a Kwakwaka'wakw Chief, Adam Dick (Kwaaksistala).

Adam had been kept back from residential school by his parents and trained as a keeper of traditional knowledge. To John's considerable gratification, Adam recalled a four-verse song, the Gilford Island version of the "Dog Skins" story, in which three boys sang of how to help their mother. One son sang of building a clam garden or, in Kwakwalla, a *lo xwi we* (pronounced "loh keh weh"). Bouchard tracked down the term *lo xwi we* in Boas's unpublished dictionary in the American Philosophical Society Collection. John reported that Bouchard had told him: "The second line of page 404 contains the word '*lo xwi we*'. One of its definitions means 'place of rolling rocks together.' Boas never understood their function."[2]

> *Walking on the sands by the sea one day, Copper Man saw clams spurting liquid of many colours. When he dug to find them, instead of clams he found little bivalve coppers, which he collected and which eventually brought him much wealth. These copper clams were carved on his staff.[3]*

John felt the existence of this term and the song was a confirmation of his speculations. The question was why had this material lain unexplored for so long? Native people agree it was mainly women who dug clams with ironwood digging sticks and wove the cedar-withe openwork backpacks in which they carried them home. Elders say that, as children accompanying their mothers and aunts, they were told to either dig clams or roll rocks to the edge of the wall. Harper speculated that the dearth of textual information about clam gardens might have something to do with the clam's association with women's work. A close examination of a live cockle will make it clear why they are associated with male genitalia, and carved wooden cockles took a spurtingly active role in the *Bukwus* ("Wild Man of the Woods") dance I saw performed in the Big House at Alert Bay. The vulvaform, found engraved in stone petroglyphs throughout the coast, resembles an edge-on view of a clam. The story of Mink and the Starfish Women is amusingly in step with this interpretation. As is the case with Nu-chah-nulth dance screens relating to the onset of a girl's menstruation, which were little noted by anthropologists, women's skills, knowledge, and ceremonies connected to sexuality, menstruation, and birthing were not made available to male anthropologists.

Despite mention of clams in a number of indigenous stories, it's possible clams were so ubiquitous in Native life they were ignored by researchers in favour of the wonder of the salmon return and its ceremonies. Salmon *are* a wonder, but a lack of rights on crucial salmon rivers, or a greater distance from their village to a spawning stream, forced some families to rely heavily on clams.

While interviewing Harper for a *Georgia Straight* article in 2002,

Terry Glavin brought to his attention Bernhard J. Stern's 1934 monograph on Lummi Natives describing a clam garden at Eleling on Orcas Island that he'd quoted in *The Last Great Sea.* "They took the largest rocks that were in the clam bed and moved them out to extreme low water marks, setting them in rows like a fence along the edge of the water," states Stern. "This made clam digging very easy compared to what it had previously been because there were only small pebbles and sand to dig in. It is exceptional to cultivate clams in this manner and while other clam beds are used by everyone in the tribe, here only the owners who cultivated the bed gathered."[4]

That beds were privately owned echoes claims by ethnobotanist Douglas Deur that land gardens at the Nimpkish River and on the Kingcome delta were privately owned and marked as such with flags.[5] Private ownership would appear to be a key to the amount of work undertaken making a clam garden.

In the summer of 2003, John and Mary took Daisy Sewid-Smith, Adam Dick and Kim Recalma-Clutesi, Randy Bouchard, and a small film crew up to the Broughton. In a filmed sequence from the subsequent film, *Ancient Sea Gardens: Mystery of the Pacific Northwest*, Mary Morris watches Adam roll a rock down a clam flat toward the wall as they discuss the belief that this task was done by women. Adam stands up, says "The big guy did this," hefts the stone, and drops it onto the wall to forcefully integrate it with other boulders.[6]

As John's group moves around the territory, Daisy explains how, when they lived on Gilford Island, her family passed their gardens down through the generations. Adam sings the Dog Skins song containing the term *lo xwi we*, finds the beach at Deep Bay his family clammed on, and tells John how a Sasquatch stole four bags of their clams.[7]

I certainly wanted to hear how a scientist slotted that Sasquatch into his data and called John. I said I knew of clam gardens — one at Shoal Harbour on Gilford Island and a number at Waiatt Bay on Quadra. John suggested I come to dinner before a clam garden talk he was giving in Victoria. As I walked through his door, he greeted me waving copies of the reports and letter I'd sent to the Archeology Branch.

"You've been tracking these things since 1993!" he laughed. My information had sat in the files the whole time he'd been searching for anyone who knew of clam gardens. Although filed with Waiatt Bay site reports, no cross indexing had ever been done. Since no one John talked to remembered my letter or calls, he had mainly searched for information about the Broughton area and had only dug out my report after I phoned. There was nothing to do but raise our glasses to the absurdity of our separate searches.

John had also invited Randy Bouchard and Dorothy Kennedy to dinner. When I was researching *High Slack*, they had generously sent detailed notes from their conversations with Rose Mitchell that had not been included in *Sliammon Life, Sliammon Lands*. "Rose was the best informant I ever had," Randy said. He'd recently unearthed an important tape-recorded conversation he had made on the Sliammon Reserve in May 1974 with Rose and Chief William Mitchell and their daughter Elizabeth Harry (Keeḵus).

In Bouchard and Kennedy's transcript of the recording, which I later received, Chief William Mitchell says: "You see, when they

Klahoose Chief William Mitchell and Rose Mitchell, early 1980s. PHOTO COURTESY MICHELLE WASHINGTON

were digging clams years ago, the old Indians didn't leave the rock there — that would be in the way for next time they would come to dig clams. They took them rocks and they kept piling them off, so that it would make it easy digging the next time they came out digging clams. That's what *wuxwuthin* was about." Then he likens the meaning of the word to the meaning of "breakwater." "You see, you take them breakwaters at Westview [south of Powell River], they're *wuxwuthin*."

Randy: "Well, '-thin' [suffix in the word *wuxwuthin*] has something to do with the mouth."

Elizabeth Harry: "Mm-hm. Well that's, see, it would make it like the mouth of the clam-bed, you know." Keeḵus and William agree *wuxwuthin* means a clam breakwater.[8]

After dinner John screened his video mapping of Waiatt Bay so I could indicate the location of the rock structures I'd seen. We compared my rock wall photographs with his. It seemed obvious we'd been looking at the same kind of constructions in two different locations.

Harper's public talk was presented as both a geographic and

intellectual journey. Shining through the graphs, charts, and beach slope diagrams of his scientific endeavours was a determination to pursue what had become for him a personally transforming vision. At the end a Haida man thanked him for his sensitive approach to the material but asked that John not continue using the term "myth" with regard to material like the "Dog Skins" song. It had, he said, acted for too long as a block to acceptance of Native people's stories as history.

As we crossed from Vancouver Island to the mainland on the ferry ride home, this new view of something ancient sent my mind racing back over the bays and old village sites we'd seen on boat journeys from Seattle to the Queen Charlotte Islands. Where else had such rock wall structures been built? What sea conditions were most productive for butter clam culture? What population densities might provoke and accomplish such labour? Recently anthropologists have suggested that early estimates of 100,000 people on the Northwest Coast had been gross underestimates.

Much seemed to hinge on the date of the walls construction and I was sure their dating would have to constitute the heart of future investigations.

In the following weeks I couldn't shake a fascination with how John and I came at the clam garden story from opposite directions. John had taken a scientifically guided roundabout to the Native knowledge platform from which Keekus had launched me. I was intrigued by the image of a curiosity-fuelled double spiraling towards a temporary meeting of minds that was accomplished only through Native verification. The form of that energizing spiral of curiosity and speculation, its meeting point and its dispersal, is as interesting to me as clam terrace construction. It illuminates how different minds and disciplines explore the world and how easily, and in what ways, depth and progression of perception can be blocked.

There is a poem by Lionel Kearns:

> At daybreak these nebulous lines gather again
> to illuminate the edge of a coastline that grows
> longer as you measure it.

"Lines For Gerri," entertains the notion that the interior of a circumstance can expand infinitely — emotionally, spiritually, and intellectually — within what appear to be finite parameters. Kearns is talking about marriage and a shared life, but perhaps he'll forgive another reading, one pertinent to John's mapping — literally *measuring* — the coast, and how his first sighting of a clam terrace exploded into a new path of knowledge and speculation.

By August 2003, both social scientists and Native groups had taken notice of this new area of information, and archeologist Kevin Robinson had undertaken a visit to the Broughton for the BC Archeological Site Inventory, in affiliation with the Nam-gis First Nation. He observed pre-contact renewable-resource activity involving what he calls petroform clam terraces on Bon-wick Island, which is at the heart of the Broughton area Harper mapped. In his official report, Robinson identifies the sites as pre-contact because, he states, they are associated with a large midden containing no historical material. His description of a Bonwick rock wall clam terrace could be a description of many clam gar-dens along the coast:

> The intertidal petroform site consists of a 40 m semi-circular wall of stacked angular boulders (20–60 cm typical), extending across the mouth of a small cove which dries at low tide. The wall is smoothly curved with the concave side facing the sea, and the base at (or below) the zero datum. The wall slopes steeply to the upper edge, about 2.5 m. The upper edge of the wall protrudes slightly above a terrace of biogentic sediment, which has filled the small cove, and slopes up gently to meet the upper intertidal natural shore-line of exposed bedrock and a low grassy bank at the head of the cove.

At the end of this site report he made a significant but careful note that verified John's proposal: "Several similar sites are visible at low tide within [an adjacent bay]. These petroform walls have apparently been constructed to trap sediment and enhance clam production."

5

Who, When, Where, and Why?

Every jigsaw picture puzzle contains pieces whose bewildering lack of definition frustrate completion. Definition of who constructed the clam gardens must remain largely speculative since no one, so far, has dated them. A temporary solution is to shift around pieces of information indicating which tribal groups lived in a territory over a sufficient span of time to have accomplished the physical work. The location reports I have received, and the clam gardens John Harper and I have personally viewed, indicate that clam cultivation existed from Orcas Island to Alaska and that the technique was used by a number of linguistic groups. However, the majority of sites observed have been within the territory of the Kwakwaka'wakw and Mainland and Island Comox peoples.

The coast from Seymour Narrows to the top of Vancouver Island, and the adjacent mainland shore, is inhabited by a large collection of Kwakwalla-speaking tribes. Some Kwakwaka'wakw ("Those who speak Kwakwalla") — the Hahuamis, the Tsawatainuk, the Gwawaenuk, the Kwiksootainuk, and at one time the Dlidliget — claim to have inhabited the area around Broughton Island since the beginning of time. An origin story from the Kwiksootainuk of Gilford Island tells of the Kulas, Mr. and Mrs. Too Large, who came as Thunderbirds to Meetup in Viner Sound, where they removed their bird masks and became human. Their sons settled in four villages around Gilford.

It was on behalf of the Kwiksootainuk that, in 1914, Chief Johnny Scow addressed the Canadian government's McKenna-McBride Royal Commission, which was charged with producing a "final adjustment of all matters relating to Indian Affairs in the Province of British Columbia." Scow petitioned for "clam stations" at Alikwis, Apsigiyu (Shoal Harbour), Islet Point, all of Bonwick Island, Kayala on Sail Island, Khwakhwakes, Echo Bay on Gilford Island, Kwita and Lixes on the Burdwood Islands, Kyimla in Tribune Channel, and Health Lagoon.[1] This is within the area that Harper says contains over 350 clam gardens. The location Kevin Robinson surveyed for the BC Archeological Site Inventory and the Namgis First Nation is on Bonwick Island.

Mamalilikala Chief Harry Mountain of Village Island claimed nearby Hakaula, Yiuyigai and Kiayas, Mataltsyu, and Tsaite (Mound Island) for clams. On a 1990 visit to Mound Island, I saw indications that a walled terrace had been built on Tsaite's northeast side.

Based on these post-contact claims, and on well-accepted claims of prehistoric occupation of this area by branches of the Kwakwaka'wakw, it can be *proposed* that Kwakwalla-speakers built those clam gardens.

Can we propose that the Waiatt Bay clam terraces were built by the Mainland Comox (comprising the Klahoose, Sliammon and Homalco) and/or the Island Comox people who occupied this area in pre-contact times? Keekus said the rock walls there were "built by our people," which I understood to mean either the Klahoose themselves or some members of the Island or Mainland Comox group. During our 1993 conversations she emphasized that the Klahoose, Sliammon, and Homalco were once one people.

Dr. Don Mitchell's 1967 site reports in the provincial archeological files note that Waiatt Bay was taken over by a Kwakwalla-speaking group, the Lekwiltok, during historical times. But he notes that, prior to European incursion on the coast, all the west side of Quadra Island and the territory north to Salmon Bay, on Vancouver Island at the bottom of Johnstone Strait and the area south to Comox Harbour appear to have been mainly under Island Comox control. The Island Comox name for Waiatt was Gayit. Little archeological work has been done in this area, so definitive pre-contact information is skimpy, but a dig at Rebecca Spit on Quadra Island uncovered a Salish fort thought to be 200 to 300 years old.

The primary textual record of the Island and Mainland Comox

comes from the journals of European explorers. A combined Spanish and British flotilla anchored in Klahoose/Sliammon territory at Kinghorn Island in Desolation Sound and then moved up Lewis Channel to the north shore of Teakerne Arm on June 26, 1792. While the British *Discovery* and *Chatham*, and the Spanish *goletas Mexicana* and *Sutil*, lay at anchor, crews explored and mapped the surrounding territory in small boats. All report the necessity of passing rapids around Stuart Island to proceed north. George Vancouver's map of the area generalizes Quadra and the surrounding islands as one mass between Stuart Island, at the mouth of accurately rendered Bute Inlet, and Vancouver Island.

After Vancouver's ships left Desolation Sound on July 13, both Vancouver and Archibald Menzies record a visit to Cape Mudge, at the southern tip of Quadra, whose hospitable villagers were Salish speakers. They visited a second Salish-speaking village in Nymphe Cove in Menzies Bay and safely traversed Seymour Narrows rapids north. Ripple Rock, which caused the treacherous boils and overfalls there, was called Ma7t'ey or "horse clam"[2] in the Island Comox dialect because it spit in the air at the race of the tide. An expedition Vancouver sent ahead up Discovery Channel

Kwakiutl Chiefs at Alert Bay, June 2, 1914. Johnny Scow is at extreme left next to Jim Humchit.
BC ARCHIVES #H-0721

to Chatham Point met with twenty canoes filled with Native people somewhere between Seymour Narrows and Elk Bay. Nearby
was the Salish-speaking settlement of Kanis on Quadra.

Travelling the eastern route north, the Spanish encountered
the Homalco, the Mainland Comox people in control of territory
from Hole in the Wall to the Southgate and Homathko Rivers at
the head of Bute Inlet. The Homalco taught them how to traverse
the tricky Arran Rapids between Stuart Island and the mainland.
When the Homalco met with the McKenna-McBride Commission in 1912, they asked for all of Bartlett Island, off Church House
just below Stuart, because a shellfish terrace east from that island
provided clams for all their people.

In 1993 *High Slack* research had led me to Robert Galois, who
was then completing *Kwawaka'waka Settlements, 1775-1920: A
Geographical Analysis and Gazetteer*. The invaluable edifice
Bob constructed on the foundation of Wilson Duff's tracking of
the territorial mobility of Kwakwalla speakers helps fit together
a number of puzzle pieces labeled "who," "when," "where," and
"why." Bob's gazetteer stresses that the tribe most relevant to
Waiatt during the post-contact period was the Kwakwalla-speaking Lekwiltok, comprising Weewiakay, Weewiakum, Tlaaluis,
Walitsma, Hahamatsees, Kweeha, and Komenox sub-groups.

Highlighting the remarkably permeable boundaries between
Kwakwalla and Salish speakers during this period, Bob writes:
"The history of the Lekwiltok tribes is complex and dramatic,
encompassing wars, mergers and divisions, the end result of
which was a significant territorial expansion." He cites the fear-
some reputation they held amongst the Coast Salish of the Gulf of
Georgia and the Puget Sound area. From origins near Nimpkish
River and Beware Passage, the Lekwiltok pushed forcefully into
Coast Salish territory, possibly even before first contact. Colonial
documentation places them in Topaz Harbour, at south end of
Johnstone Strait, the descent site of their culture hero Wiakay.
There is a low pass from Jackson Bay, off Topaz Harbour, into
Glendale Cove in Knight Inlet where the Kweeha had oolichan
rights. Some Lekwiltok fished oolichan in Bute Inlet in 1862, but
that and the Klahoose's Toba Inlet run soon failed. Loss of such a
key food resource could have necessitated an expansion of territory and alternate food-production systems like clam gardens.

Searching for reasons for the Lekwiltok's move south, Galois

Homalco,
"Village of
the Friendly
Indians at
the Entrance
to Bute's
Canal, 1792."
*Engraving
from George
Vancouver,*
A Voyage of
Discovery
to the North
Pacific Ocean
and Around
the World
1791–1795.

cites the socially disruptive 1782 smallpox epidemic, which devastated Salish groups to a greater degree than it did the Lekwiltok. He notes that "ecological and consequent social differences made Coast Salish vulnerable to northern raids." The Namgis people at Nimpkish River on Vancouver Island possessed muskets (observed by Captain Vancouver in 1792) that they obtained from their involvement in the lucrative fur trade taking place on the west coast and northwest tip of Vancouver Island during the 1700s. With few otter pelts to trade, the Salish missed this economic and armament boom and were vulnerable to an armed group like the Lekwiltok.

From the 1830s the Lekwiltok claimed territory west of Waiatt, and, according to elders Peter Smith and James Henderson, their Kwakwalla name for Waiatt was Wayad, "a place that has herring." By 1850 Weewiakay/Weewiakum territory encompassed Vancouver Island from Chatham Point to south of Campbell River. Their control of Quadra Island, centred within the sets of rapids that must be traversed to move north or south, gained them significant control over movement through the Inside Passage. However, for the most part Read, Sonora, the Redonda Islands and the territories east remained the possessions of Klahoose and Homalco people. Although the Weewiakum occupied five different sites, sometimes concurrently, by the last quarter of the nineteenth century, most lived at Campbell River.

Confused? Even Boas wrote that, with regard to the Lekwiltok,

"I had no success in differentiating the territory of these five tribes because they all live in each village except the Wiweaqams."[3]

Let me arrange these fragments differently. It's thought the original Salish inhabitants of the north end of Quadra Island were called Tatapoos,[4] and Tatapowis, or T'at apa'uyas in Salish, was the Maurelle Island village in Whiterock Passage I passed on my first trip to Waiatt. The name is variously translated as "place that becomes dry," "big boulders going dry," or "the flood when canoes can be launched." The village appears to have been captured by some Lekwiltok in the early 1830s. The combined Weewiakay/Weewiakum sub-groups lived there together until the Weewiakay moved to Discovery Passage just before 1835 (although some remained at Tatapowis into the 1880s). A section of the Weewiakay split off and became the Walitsma and moved to Salmon River, which belonged to the Hahamatsees, an Island Comox group. A Campbell River Museum dig indicates that two linguistic groups with different style canoes may have lived there together, but the Walitsma assumed control between 1865 and 1880. Displaced Tatapoos may have moved to Mushkin (Old Church House), outside Hole In the Wall on Sonora Island, or to Chichxwiyakalh on south Stuart Island.

In Juan de Fuca Strait Captain Valdes took on board the Mexicana *a local chieftain Tetacus who accompanied them north to his settlement of Cordoba. There his people "presented Valdes with some fruit, like figs in shape, black, and of a floury character, with a salt taste.*[5]

Tatapowis was also used by the Lekwiltok Kweeha sub-group after they moved from Matsayno in Phillips Arm and before they went on to Matltum in Cardero Channel in 1875. Interestingly, Galois notes that the origin place of the Kweeha was Wahkana Bay, in Tribune Channel, off Broughton territory. I jigged for cod there at Clam Point, off a small, tidal island clam bed. The Kweeha had also occupied Tsaite, the two-tiered Mound Island village which Chief William Glendale of nearby Tzatsisnukomi told me had been abandoned due to lack of water.

Indian Reserve Commissioner G.M. Sproat allocated a village site, adjacent gardens, and a burial ground at Tatapowis to the Weewiakum around 1870. Wilson Duff noted the village was burned shortly before 1886, and the Weewiakum also moved to Matltun. In 1888 Kweeha Chief Lalakinnis said Tatapowis "was not wanted as the salmon did not run there now."[6] In 1900, when remains of a fortified village were still visible, Commissioner Powell allotted Tatapowis to the Klahoose, although it was acknowledged to properly be a Homalco reserve.

The Tlaaluis from Phillips Arm were closely related to the Kweeha and said to be mainly Salish in language, ritual, and custom. They took over the Homalco hunting and fishing site Saaiyouck at the Arran Rapids and were attacked there by either the Bella Bella or a Salish party. In 1873 the Kweeha lived there, and by 1887 they had three houses and a chum salmon fishing station. By 1910 the Kweeha had joined the Weewiakay at Cape Mudge. Susan Pielle told me the Klahoose Mitchell family stayed at some old shacks at Saaiyouck in the 1950s and she was able to pick the sea urchins she liked to eat nearby.

Galois indicates the peripatetic Weewiakum moved from Tatapowis to Waiatt Bay, which they called Gayat (and knew to have been an Island Comox name and site), before they moved north to Matltun near Loughborough Inlet. The Weewiakum scarcely seem to have been in situ long enough to construct the extensive Waiatt terraces.

Near that time the Weewiakay moved into Kanish Bay. Mungo Martin mentioned a village on the north side of the bay, possibly Kan'is village just north of Small Inlet, although, according to Galois, there are the remains of sixteen villages of some antiquity within the larger bay. Salish speakers continued using what Weewiakay Harry Assu identifies as a herring and berry-picking station into 1840. He says four Lekwiltok groups lived there together.

This rapidly shifting picture suggests that Tatapowis was desirable throughout most of this tumultuous period due to its defending rock pile, its on-site clam beds, and the productive fishery in Surge Narrows and the surrounding rapids. Salish speakers were ousted from Tatapowis and chum fishing stations at Saaiyouck so Lekwiltok could obtain these food sources. Nevertheless, until Waiatt clam terrace construction can be dated, it's impossible to say with certainty if Island Comox constructed the clam gardens and the sites later fell to Mainland Comox, or vice versa, or if the intruding Lekwiltok carried the technique south with them. All user groups may have contributed to considerably older structures. Waiatt is, however, the most concentrated clam complex so far seen.

None of this addresses what population density would lead to the massive resource constructed at Waiatt since we have only guesstimates of pre-contact population numbers. Galois favours Dr. W.F. Tolmie's 1830 estimates based on twenty-five people per old-style house. This suggests 125 Weewiakum within a Lekwiltok population of 1,100. A later conjecture proposes forty-five people per house, and another speculator fancifully bases his count on the number of bearded men. It seems unlikely that only 125 people would have been able to build the Waiatt walls during their brief tenure.

If we shift direction and consider the clam gardens to be truly ancient, it's useful to note that extensive digs at Namu dating back 9,000 years indicate different kinds of protein were consumed during different eras, with a clam/salmon mix following the earliest period of sea mammal consumption. Harper suggests that in Broughton middens, a lower level of residue from surface-collectable mussels and barnacles underlies a denser upper layer of clam shell, a change that might indicate the beginning of clam terrace construction. If more butter clams were consumed, what caused the switch? Had the mussels died off, become infected, or been over-harvested? Perhaps people saw the possibility for a productive new technology as beaches were used for a variety of reasons.

It is significant that butter clams, like salmon, preserve remarkably well, and it's thought the dried floury "fruits" Cayetano Valdes was given by Tetacus's people in 1792 were smoked clams. It is an accepted anthropological theory that the ability to preserve food led to the accumulation by coastal people of goods and food available to be given away at winter potlatches. The complex society encountered by the explorers may not have existed before the storage, trade, and feasting that oolichan grease, dried salmon, and clam production allowed. But coastal conditions vary, and while some families controlled large salmon and oolichan resources, others did not, and it may have been in such areas, as around Gilford Island, that clams were heavily cultivated.

In *Peoples of the Northwest Coast: Their Archeology and Prehistory*, written prior to clam garden research, Kenneth Ames and Herbert Maschner address the issue of dietary change.[7] They state that in the Pacific period (6350 to 3750 YBP) there is a marked increase in the use of intertidal resources. They cite K.R. Fladmark, who attributed this to an "indirect result of the stabilization

of sea levels at their current positions at 3800 BC [5750 YBP]."
Fladmark believes sea-level stabilization led to increased use of
salmon. This, in turn, led to increased sedentism, or living at one
place all year round, and this led to increased use of molluscs.
Ames and Mascher counter that the development from pit houses,
such as the Klahoose occupied in Toba before European contact,
to large plank houses led to settling and exploitation of mollusks.
They focus on the technological invention of the plank house as
a big storage container containing the smaller storage-box unit
within. They also make the significant point that shellfish could
be gathered by women, children, and the aged, which increased
the workforce supplying protein for the group.

Is there a reason to eat clams if salmon is available? Butter clams
could be harvested in the winter, when salmon three times a day
started to pall, but clams also provide higher amounts of carbo-
hydrate than fish — 26.8 grams per pound compared to o grams
per pound from chum salmon. Dried clams dipped in oolichan
grease provided a spectacular balance of protein, carbohydrates,
and Omega 3 oil.

The requests to the Indian Reserve Commission for reserve
lands connected to clam stations beyond village sites indicate the
value placed on clams even in historic times. Neither the Reserve
Commission officers, nor those undertaking archeological investigations or clam inventories, understood that Native people were
asking for nutritionally valuable, cultivated and family-owned
beds. The subsequent focus on salmon as the sole engine of all
Native groups on the coast skewed understanding of Native economy. Although experts disagree about the development of sedentism, clam cultivation, consumption, processing, and clam garden
ownership now seem important nutritional and economic aspects
of some areas of cultural growth and will have to be incorporated
into any new theoretical writing.

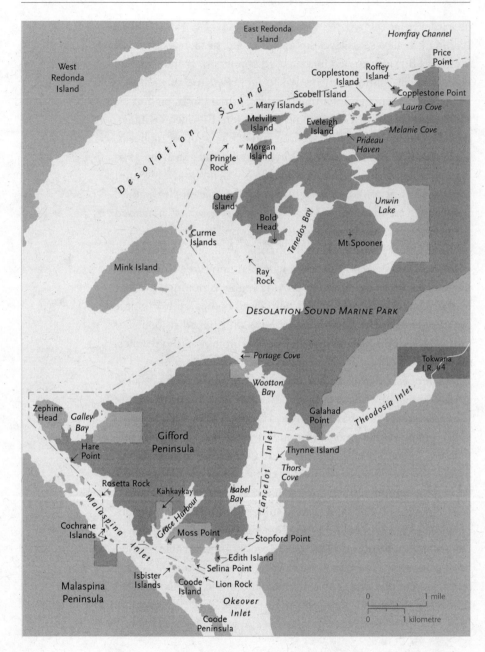

Malaspina Inlet to Desolation Sound. Lighter shaded areas within Desolation Sound Marine Park are private.

6

Other Directions

The accumulating data about Waiatt Bay clam gardens, John's story of those in the Broughton, the reported Orcas Island structures, and news that Linda Hogarth, curator of the Campbell River Museum, had found eleven clam benches in Kanish Bay on the northwest side of Quadra was exciting. I began to consider where clam terraces might have been developed in Mainland Comox territory around my home port at Refuge Cove in Desolation Sound. If any of this group, or the related Island Comox, built the Waiatt or Kanish terraces, one might expect similar structures in other parts of their territory — although, given Keekus's insistence that Waiatt produced the "best clams," in less-productive configurations. Clam garden location, layout, and form appeared to be related to village proximity, population density, nutrient conditions, local geography, and observation of the success of other complexes. I remembered that the Mainland Comox village of Kahkaykay, at Grace Harbour in Malaspina Inlet, fulfilled some of those conditions, and it had a boulder-edged clam flat.

My earliest boating adventure southeast of Desolation Sound had been a 1988 expedition to Kahkaykay, the unoccupied Sliammon Indian Reserve #6, next to Grace Harbour Marine Park in Malaspina. Named after the Parmesan captain Alejandro Malaspina, who travelled the coast in the 1790s for Spain, the inlet stretches south from Desolation to marshy flats at the end of Okeover Arm. On the southwest shore, opposite a set of pictographs, is a dock marking the north end of any public road beyond the coastal highway's terminus at Lund.

Grace Harbour lies on the southwest end of Malaspina's Gifford Peninsula, and Kahkaykay occupies land in the middle of three bays within the harbour. It had caught my eye when I read in *Sliammon Life, Sliammon Lands* that it was the location of Sliammon, Klahoose, and Homalco winter ceremonials. In the 1930s, Klahoose Chief Julian recalled the erection there of four twelve-metre memorial poles. The Grace Harbour marine park survey noted that elders told Sliammon advisor Norm Gallagher that boards now weathered out of the village midden were from a Big House that once stood here. The village continued to be occupied until the 1960s.

On our 1988 excursion we anchored the boat and walked up a cleared path below the village site. My companion, Hannes Grosse, walked behind the cabin, still used by Sliammon clam diggers working this site, and down into a drained, rock-rimmed basin. He picked up a stone spearhead, turned, bent, and found a faceted blue trade bead. Here was material evidence of both pre- and post-contact occupation. On a subsequent occasion I wandered the basin looking for some permanent evidence of ancient

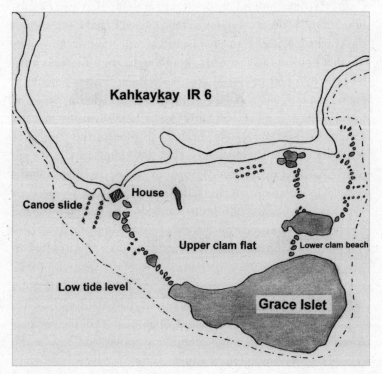

Kaykaykay complex.

occupation, but I did not then realize I was standing on the living artifact I sought.

Sixteen years later, in 2004, one of the lowest tides of the year was predicted for June 3. I headed *Tac* across a mirror-smooth Desolation Sound and into Malaspina to take a more informed look at Grace Harbour. I pulled up short just south of the inlet's entrance, at Hare Point, when I saw the two rock walls that curved out from the shore to a tidal island were high out of the water. The foreshore had definitely been built up to extend, level, and stabilize a clam flat. My friend Walter Franke had clammed for a living quite some time in Malaspina, and I had to consider whether Walter, or the other non-Native shellfish growers in Malaspina, might have altered beaches here. Was this their work or that of indigenous people? I could only be confident this was a pre-contact structure if I knew when it was built. I did know from previous observation that contemporary Klahoose people dug and sold clams from this spot, and I was sure that, even though littleneck and butters would grow at some level in such a bed, the majority of their harvest would be the market-favoured Manilas.

> The Tl'uhus people made a conscious effort to cultivate clean clam beds. As they dug clams, the people removed the rocks from the gravel and piled them on one edge of the beach or in the water beyond the mark of the lowest tide. These piles of rocks are called wuxwuthin, "held back at the mouth."[1]

According to an archeological site report, Hare Point contained a "fish trap," "canoe skids," and 170 metres of midden. The canoe slides made sense; the "fish trap" now looked to be a still-active clam garden.

Farther south in the inlet I rounded Kakaekae Point into Grace Harbour and nosed *Tac* into a slick of water over soft muck at the base of the western line of boulders at Kahkaykay. The orderliness and convenience of the abrupt drop-off into the water along this long rock pile now seemed considered rather than fortuitous. When I walked up from the water between the parallel lines comprising what I now recognized as a canoe slide, I could see how boulders were purposely placed to connect bedrock outcrops from there to Grace Islet, which was said to be used as a podium during the ceremonials. Within two slightly curved rock arms out to the islet lay a flat, lightly pebbled basin. Faint mounds and hollows

Kahkaykay
upper clam
terrace.

indicated recent digging, and my shallow scrape revealed littlenecks and Manilas in such abundance that they'd pushed each
other up to the surface.

Slightly below that flat basin, a line of boulders swung north
from Grace Islet. Contained within rock lines was thick butter
clam hash, punctuated by semi-buried boulders. Loose Pacific
oysters were scattered atop these lower beds, though they would
not have been there before their 1920s introduction. As I inserted
a garden fork to dig for clams, I hit boulders and, around them, at
twenty-five centimetres below the surface, six- to eight-centimetre
butters.

Although I could not ascertain the depth of the hash, which was
prime butter clam habitat, it was certainly intriguing to consider
how long it might take to attain the kind of density I saw here
and in the clam gardens at Waiatt Bay. All village middens contain masses of clam shells, indicating that huge numbers of clams
were carried back to the villages, but the density of clam hash on
beaches like this suggests many clams were steamed and opened
right where they were dug.

The double terracing indicated villagers had outlined separate
beds to encourage different kinds of clams based on their knowledge of the conditions in which various species thrive. Both terraces lay below the abrupt rise to the plateau where houses had
stood and which was now a tangle of tall grass, fruit trees, and

blackberry vines frequented by bears. Pot hunters had dug pockets into the south face of this rise, from which high winter tides eroded the shell-studded blue/black soil so characteristic of old villages.

We climbed back into *Tac* and cruised into the inner bay of Grace Harbour, which is the marine park, and landed on a beach at the head of the bay's right lobe. Here butter clam shells dotted the lower beach level, which rose sharply up to a wide, drained flat that was bracketed by abrupt cliffs. I tied the boat to the only protuberance, a strikingly cubist-shaped stone midway between the two levels. Sharp-faceted rocks flanked the lightly pebbled centre of the upper beach, which surface was as even and flat as a ballroom floor. A few clam shells indicated littlenecks and Manilas grew there. We sat at the base of the cliffs, eating our lunch, and contemplated the origin of this remarkable planar equality. At the head of the bay, where a blue flag marked a trail inland, was a 1.5-metre-high barrier of boulders, similar in size to those composing the Waiatt walls. It did seem, as Rose Mitchell had said, that in this territory clam beds were cleared by boulders being moved up, to the side, or to the sea edge of the beach.

Lunch consumed, we headed south out of Grace Harbour and turned east inside Lion Rock toward Edith Island. According to Bouchard and Kennedy's 1974 notes of conversations with Rose Mitchell, "two of the major clam digging areas were on the southeast end of Gifford Island [presumably Gifford Peninsula] between Edith Island and Stopford Point as you turn north east into Lancelot Inlet. The rocky reef off Stopford Point is called Kwikwnach. When you are digging here while the tide is going out, you can follow along the beach from the shore to Edith Island, called *tatihapten* — 'follow the beach'."

Rose states that the tool used to dig in this territory was a metre-long ironwood or yew stick called *kayax*, although a large horse clam shell could be used in soft sand, and clams were "carried home in an open work basket" called *yaxay*.[2]

The bay west of Edith Island was now full of oyster farm gear, and at this low tide it was connected by a berm to the island. A canoe slide crossed this berm, and both sloped down to a clam flat in the bay to the east. A submerged bedrock rise and several large rocks near the mainland shore contained that beach, so no wall was needed. Clam hash dotted with butter clam shells extended below datum on both sides of the neck-like berm.

Stopford Point (Kwikwnach) is less than a kilometre north of Edith Island, and just west of the point itself is a fish trap. A low wall of sharp rocks spans the narrow entrance to a level basin that is cleared of big rocks and full of horse, butter, and littleneck shells. There is a gap in the centre of the wall where a basket fish trap could be secured — or the opening closed with rocks once fish had entered the basin. Behind the offshore tidal bedrock, the point is laced by a series of low boulder lines completely filled with clam hash. Lying on the surface were the largest butter clam shells I'd yet seen. There was no obvious outer wall to this beach. The seasonal campsite above, used by people processing fish and shellfish, is a handsome bluff with arbutus trees leaning out over tall grass.

I cruised *Tac* farther up Lancelot Inlet and east into the entrance of Theodosia Inlet. At the tide change water rushes in or out of the inner basin like a river. Clam hash lies within what might be either a hand-built or current-created wall on the north side.

A log dump is fed by a road curving left, then right, towards the hidden mouth of the Theodosia River. At low tide, the innermost bay dries out for over a kilometre from the river, which runs for kilometres from the flat Olsen Valley. It was once one of the great salmon rivers of the coast, providing sustenance for the population at Toquana village here. That run began to disappear after the river was dammed in 1924 to raise water levels on Powell Lake

Stopford Point
fish trap.

Stopford Point clam flat, behind the fish trap.

and provide power for the Powell River pulp mill, and the village was abandoned. There have been efforts by Mark Angelo of the Outdoor Recreation Council to restore its salmon run.

I turned at the weathered pictograph on the south shore of a small island where a now-submerged, semicircular fish trap connects island to mainland. *Tac* bucked the inflowing tide bubbling through the neck of Theodosia Inlet out to Lancelot Inlet. At the junction of the inlets, Wooten Bay opens north/northeast to the narrow neck of Portage Cove, which connects Gifford Peninsula to the mainland. A fish trap is said to extend from a Wooten Bay islet to the mainland.

Farther west out of Lancelot Inlet we turned north past the Isbister Islands, between which there is also said to be a fish trap. These three sets of fish traps could prove also to be clam gardens, but would have to await examination on another low tide. As we headed north out of Malaspina, the flood boiled in through the narrows with considerable force and flushed the commercial abalone and oyster farms and the clam beds with the nutrients that make the area an excellent shellfish environment.

Theodosia's former enormous salmon run, the inlet's protected waters and many habitable sites, suggest that a fair-sized pre-contact population could have occupied Malaspina. I knew from friends who'd tilled it for a market garden in the 1970s that all of the Portage Cove isthmus was an extremely deep midden and a game trail from the mainland to the more open areas of Gifford Peninsula. Portage's outer bay, facing Desolation, drained to a long shallow flat. Once, during one of those dark, inconvenient, winter low tides, the caretaker there decided to harvest some of the flat's abundant clams. He set a Coleman lantern on the sand to shed some light on his activities and, busy with his work, only looked up when its beam was broken by a cougar strolling past.

No archeological work has been done at Portage Cove, but I once peered down into an illegal 1.5-metre hole someone had dug in the midden. I could see the densely layered remains of a diet of clams and occasional mussels, relieved by snacks of the spiny urchins growing below datum on Rosario Rock, inside the entrance narrows.

My Malaspina expedition indicated the Sliammon constructed several kinds of clam beds, but I'd seen no *complex* of terraces matching Waiatt's constructions. However, in areas such as this, which were settled relatively early by Europeans, one must factor in the extensive shoreline modification by homesteaders, loggers, and even Natives meeting the market's shifting clam needs.

According to Rose Mitchell, the Klahoose knew Corbey's Beach in Lewis Channel, north of Malaspina, as Xa7am or "having clams."[3] Shellfish-cultivating pals who work in this area tell of a contemporary dispute about a Lewis Channel beach that was given over to a commercial clam lease, but is currently claimed by the Klahoose as a long-time clam station. Xa7am?

I was interested in locating evidence that the Klahoose, as well as the Sliammon, used the clam garden technology I had seen in the Waiatt Bay terraces, and it was details such as this that led me to follow what I thought might be another clue from Rose in *Sliammon Life, Sliammon Lands* that "the only clam beach in Toba Inlet" is at Snout Point (*i'wu7ulh* or "stepping stone"). Snout Point is on the south shore of the mainland, where Toba Inlet bends northeast to the abruptly rising Coast Range.

In 1987, Klahoose Chief Danny Louie, Helen and Larry Hanson, elder Joe Barnes (who had been raised in Toba), Sliammon Chief Roy Francis, and I had cruised up Toba to examine Klahoose reserve land, a grave site, and remnants of the permanent winter villages the Klahoose once had on five rivers flowing to the inlet's mouth. The only break in the sheer walls of the inlet, and the only relatively safe shelters, are the Brem (Salmon) River bay and an area west of the single inlet islet, which anthropologist Erna Gunther said was where Spanish explorers found the unique *tabla*,[4] carved with the Klahoose clan animal, mountain goats. The Klahoose people, travelling the inlet in canoes, stopped near the islet, and I thought Snout Point, west of the islet, might contain a nearby food source. If so, it would be, indisputably, in Klahoose territory.

The tide is seldom low when you want it to be, but the tide book predicted an almost zero slack near noon on July 4, 2004. I headed up Toba with experienced boater George Pryce, who had read Stephen Hume's *Vancouver Sun* article on Harper's Broughton investigations and wanted to see a clam garden for himself. However, I was unsure if this clam bed, which friends at the Tork Reserve could not recall, would be a constructed terrace.

It was calm and sunny as we cruised up Waddington Channel between East and West Redonda Islands, but as we entered Toba Inlet, *Tac* suddenly banged into the inlet's regular afternoon chop, and jade waves began to pile up rough on Snout Point. But — there was an exposed clam bed!

Clam gardens examined by Judith Williams:

Grief Point, Westview, Sliammon Village, Hu'hjuusim, Copeland Islands, Hare Point, Grace Harbour, Edith Island, Stopford Point, Prideaux Haven, Snout Point, Gorge Harbour, Rendezvous Island, Aupe (Church House), Waiatt Bay, Kanish Bay, Cameleon Harbour, Loughborough Inlet, Port Harvey, Etsekin, Shoal Harbour, Joe Cove, Monday Anchorage, Mound Island, Wilson Passage area, Codville Lagoon.

I'd fished this point at high slack, and assumed the walls simply dropped straight down to the eighty-eight fathoms indicated on the chart. Now I could see what appeared to be a short, straight, boulder wall, facing west out into the chop between an outcrop and the tall cliff on the inlet's south side. The outcrop itself, a rock known to the Klahoose as one of the "Four Brothers" or "Four Pillars," sloped down towards the head of the inlet. It was rocky but calmer in behind.

After fussing a bit I brought the excellent *Tac* into the up-inlet shore, past sharp rocks leaping out of a chop as opaque as a frappuccino, and along what I prayed was a cleared way in. George jumped off onto slimy rocks and held the boat as I climbed onto a real oddity. Ahead, between the outcrop or "brother" and the cliff, was a cleared, beach dotted with medium-sized clam shells. Midway across this area, the ground rose and was so dense with small indigo mussels that across the middle of the entire beach, from the mainland cliff to outcrop, they covered every surface in high loose clusters. Down the west side of this rise was a cleared area sloping gently to where the beach dropped abruptly into the sea along the straight line of boulders from the outcrop to the mainland cliff. The sea was so choppy and opaque I couldn't see the depth of the wall. Turning back, facing north towards the head of the inlet, I could see random cobble at the base of the mainland cliff, and farther back, past the boat, sharp rocks poked up out of agitated kelp. There was nothing else. The exposed area was equivalent to a medium-sized Waiatt Bay terrace — not more than eighteen metres long and ten and a half metres wide. What appeared to be a boulder wall at the west end might have been built across the gap between cliff and outcrop to stop erosion caused by the sharp afternoon seas.

At this low tide, the long sandy golden flat extending out from Brem River was clearly visible across the channel. I'd seen the size of that sand bar increase after recent logging, but some silt would always have washed across from the river and from the eroding sand cliffs behind Tzella (Emerald) Creek to the south. After the wall was formed, more material would have accrued from clam shell breakdown and the hump in the middle formed by wave action.

Snout Point clam garden, facing up inlet.

A fine pictograph of an eagle lifting a humpbacked salmon is painted near a set of figures on a ledge north of the Brem River, which was known as Kw'ikw'tichenam, "having lots of pink (humpback) salmon."

In *The Coast Salish of B.C.*, Homer Barnett claims that prior to white exploration, the isolated Klahoose seldom ventured out of the inlet farther than Brem and were not really "saltwater people." It's his controversial opinion that the winter ceremonial gatherings at Grace Harbour were a later development

*Snout Point
clam garden,
west edge.*

because, he concludes, the Klahoose, Sliammon and Homalco "were not related in the way required by aboriginal pattern." He says Hwookam (Yay K Wum's father?) was the first Chief to establish full-time residence at the Brem, and he did so around 1820 in stockaded, above-ground houses. This was possibly the village Yay K Wum took Robert Homfray to in 1863 after rescuing him in Bute. Barnett's informant, Chief Julian, observed there had been so little pre-contact Kwakiutl influence that "Kwakiutl-derived masks and dances [acquired through marriage] had hardly begun to be understood by his people when governmental measures for the suppression of their use began to be effective circa 1920."[5]

According to Klahoose history, two of the Snout Point outcrop's "brothers" are the large boulder at Squirrel Cove and the much-graffitied big rock below Campbell River. Ken Hanuse of Tork suggested Hernando Island as the location of the fourth. Chief Ollie Chickite of Cape Mudge says his Klahoose mother told him the brothers are the "Four Pillars" of the Mainland and Island Comox. It isn't clear if the concept of the "Four Brothers" or "Pillars" was the backbone of an early or a later extended Island and Mainland Comox grouping, if they marked tribal boundaries or were simply a form of indicator rock marking food sources or a resource camp, such as Tork once was.

Next day I phoned Randy Bouchard, who confirmed that Rose told him the location of the Snout Point clam bed. When I said I thought the wall was placed to stop erosion, he said Tsimshian

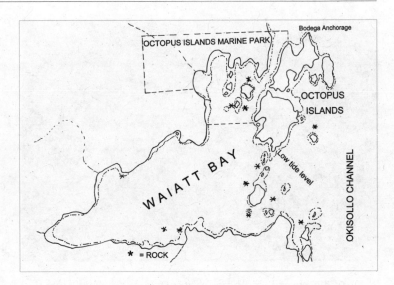

Waiatt Bay.

friends in Prince Rupert territory thought their people had built rock walls to stop waves from washing beaches away. Stone-wall technology stories had begun to arrive from many locations up the coast.

A tide book, sheaves of marine charts, and site reports became my bedside reading as I plotted expeditions to other possible clam garden locations. Technical data collided with differing positions of observation and kinds of understanding. A survey from the air is different from digging clams. When you *read* about my Toba trip you can't feel the wind and waves and are unconcerned about the amount of gas in the tanks or pushing the prop into the rocky chop far from home. Imagine being in a cedar canoe and halting after a long paddle up the inlet to roast clams on the fire before the next day-long paddle home. The Klahoose place names that Rose Mitchell's son Joe had told me about in 1993 were all about how to get to and from Toba and what there was, and was not, to eat en route. Naturally.

On July 5, Bobo and I left Refuge Cove in *Tac* and beat up Lewis Channel into the wind to traverse Hole in the Wall just before a noon low tide. We were equipped with an annotated marine chart made by John Harper's University of Victoria student Erica Beauchamp for her essay "Aboriginal Clam Gardens of the Broughton

Archipelago and Waiatt Bay, Quadra Island." Using a pause mechanism on John's 1995 video of Waiatt Bay, they'd counted and plotted rock walls and terraces, and Erica had estimated their size and compared them to those in the Broughton. Since the tide had not been at its lowest the day they'd shot the video, the terraces were not all as distinct as the lower-tide footage from Broughton, but Erica's chart indicated there were a remarkable thirty-one clam gardens in this bay. I was curious about ones I'd missed, and on this July day a very useful 0.2-metre mid-day tide was predicted.

Passage west into Okisollo from Hole in the Wall was as placid as could be expected, and I slid us across a vast silver salver engraved with salty whirls, tendrils, and blossoming boils four and a half metres wide. Occasionally a two-metre vortex swirled down what one might suppose to be the drain to the other side of the world.

We entered Bodega Anchorage where, in 1938, pictograph hunter Francis Barrow took a sweet photo of the old folks and dogs who ran a store there full of old traps and top hats. Now occupying that spot was the finest garbage scow on the coast. Flowers bloomed and flags waved as the ebbing tide revealed the scow was flanked by clam gardens. Yes! There was one on Erica's chart.

I verified the location of the series of clam gardens that Erica's map indicated were just inside the entrance to Waiatt Bay. Interestingly, on June 7, 2001, senior government archeologist Donald N. Abbott visited Waiatt to look at this spot. He was prompted by information from archeologist, Bjorn Simonson, that an elderly Sliammon woman had told him this exact area contained clam terraces. Abbott identifies these sites as fish traps, but he appends a careful coda that they might be "artificially crested clam beds."

The complex Abbott noted spans the shallow gap between North Octopus Island, South Octopus Island, and an unnamed islet. The North Octopus Island ledge has a pronounced lip that could function as a fish trap, but I'd been told it was precisely this productive shellfish area that was used by local Native and non-Native clam diggers. Abbott also notes that west of the islet there is a shell midden lying between two creeks and that this site was likely not a permanent winter village but a food gathering and processing site associated with the fish traps he found. Erica's map indicates there is a clam terrace at least 250 metres long extending southwest from that site. Abbott remarks that all the fish-trap areas are now filled in, precluding their use as fish traps. He identifies the area as "Lekwiltok; formerly Comox."

We moved farther into Waiatt and tucked into a deep V-shaped bay at the southwest side of South Octopus Island. A raccoon raised his black mask to inspect us but, more interested in edibles, continued feeling under the boulders comprising the wall that stretched in a line between two high cliffs. Leaving him to his foraging, we circled the whole big bay, checking Erica's map. Abbott's site reports make no mention of any other Waiatt Bay terraces, but nosing around at the lowest tide we'd ever seen here, it now became evident any place that could be built up was terraced — except at four spots where the sand sloped gently and naturally down around a drainage. I began to wonder what "natural" meant when at least two waves of people had rearranged some parts of this landscape to enhance their situation.

The clam terrace complex again struck me as extraordinary. It was exciting to finally see the sheer size of the benches on the south side. The dead-flat surface of one, centred around a huge boulder, arced out into the bay in an elegant curve that reversed and flipped its tail in a concave sweep shoreward. The quantity and the elegance of many installations, as well as the labour involved, was stunning.

North, across the bay, a mink raced east from Log Dump Bay along the length of a huge bench I'd not seen before. Siphon holes and empty butter clam shells dotted the surface and I decided to explore the shellfish possibilities. I struck two giant cockles, a handful of tiny bent-nose macoma clams, and a lot of empty shells before, twenty-five centimetres down, I unearthed several large butter clams. My family would not survive long on this haul. What was going on? It had been severely dry all winter and spring, and clams will move up or down in response to drought or freezing. Were the butters deeper?

We went along to the bay I landed on in 1993. A second mink scampered up the rocks. Although there was evidence of recent digging, I scored few clams. A handsome floathouse was settled down on the easternmost flank of the clam garden, and boom logs splayed out over the terrace. That was the kind of usage that would compact the beds and threaten the integrity of the walls.

Discouraged by unproductive digging and by snapping photos

that always showed a stretch of bumpy green laver that people refused to believe were actual walls, we tied to a small dock against the cliff at Raccoon Bay to eat our sandwiches. The fossicking coon had been replaced by a reddish mink who hurried down the beach and along the front of the forty centimetres of exposed wall to dig out tidbits. We almost always saw mink on clam gardens, so the stories of Mink and the tides made wonderful sense.

I decided I'd better dig some more before the *lo xwi we* or *wux-wuthin* disappeared. I dug near where tiny paw marks in the sand indicated the raccoon had foraged, and brought up butter clams, a cockle, and, with some effort, a large horse clam. The area near the cliff was full of them, and as I examined the profusion of dead butter clams in and around each horse clam, they unkindly spurted up my legs. The live butters I found were small in relation to the size of the empty shells.

No one would have built such a complex for this low level of butter clam production, although horse clams were abundant. As in any garden, productivity was enhanced by cultivation, and these beds, no longer deeply worked for butters, had silted up. I swam out into the shallow bay beyond the wall, over pure white clam hash and the blades of the brown laver used for protecting dug clams and steaming food. The tide finally slid over the top of the wall, which had been out of the water for close to three hours. We had seen forty clam terraces.

We picked our way through the kelp-choked southern entrance and headed to the Surge. I hoped to photograph the Antonio Point pictographs I'd located with Hilary Stewart and Joy Inglis. Instead we slid south along water running downhill through the Surge at a tremendous clip and out into the boils and whirlpools of the bay. There are reported to be pictographs on the cliff in the Surge proper, but I'm not sure when it's flat enough to view them.

We'd once boiled through that passage to find an Orca family had done the same. The great bull, three metres longer than *Tac*, lolled in mid-bay as the girls foraged at the current-churned shore. When he disappeared we drifted crosswise in Hoskyns Channel, and as I stood up to pour tea from a thermos for my companions, I saw three fins heading straight at us. I froze mid-pour. First, second, and third rise, up came three female Orcas, one at a time. They'd shifted direction slightly so each rolled forward parallel to

the gunnel, eyes open, had a look, and rolled forward and down tight beside the boat. The Orcas were in the Surge basin because fish were feeding there in a nutrient-rich environment near what might be the most concentrated clam-production location on the coast. One could understand this territory's desirability as a strategic location and food basket and the pressure in the late 1800s to take it under control.

Orcas would have avoided the shallow passage we took this day through Whiterock Passage and east beyond Tatapowis to locate pictographs we had seen in 1997. Curious crosses on the lower cheeks of red, boulder-shaped heads gave the personages in these paintings the appearance of the plump, dimpled Salish faces that Keekus and Susan joked attracted Chilcotin lads. Was that a scarlet arm up in greeting or warning?

I see pictographs and petroglyphs as a sign of the mind at work in what, if Native mariculture is as extensive as it seems, I can no longer completely refer to as *wild*erness. Although Pacific rock art employs a visual language I have yet to really master, variants of it can be found all over the world. When studying the oral culture of this coast, it is a valuable addition to recorded data.

Most pictographs are painted on stone cliffs kept whitish by a natural mineral flow that inhibits the black lichen growth normally found on rock. If correctly applied, the pigment is bound into the stone permanently by the mineral flow. Petroglyphs, which some observers consider much older and differently motivated, are engraved into intertidal boulders or outcrops.

Casual observers tend to view pictographs as pictures of some-

thing that resembles an object or process they know. But some
rock art is tribal sign: a stylistic bear rendered on a cliff says "This
is *our* river," and some, like those I analyzed in *Two Wolves at the
Dawn of Time*, note potlatches or specific family events. Others
are residue of shamanic activity or spirit quests and may be quite
hidden. I have seen accurate images of fish entering a salmon weir
and clusters of red lines archeologists call tally marks. Some sets of
marks combine to speak of something more intangible.

*Waiatt Bay
clam terrace,
July 2004.*

But why look for pictographs or petroglyphs near clam gardens
if the images do not directly relate to clams? It is the practice of
some observers and writers on coastal Native material, to focus on
separate aspects of indigenous usage of the landscape, or of a territory, as if they could be separated from the whole cultural fabric.
One can find a notation about the use of a salmon river that says
little more than that Native people fished there. But one has to
consider how they travelled there, the camping situation, equipment and clothes, and how they processed the fish to keep it over
the winter. Salmon habitat will always be adjacent to, or on the
route from villages, food or material sources. Cedar is needed for
canoes, clothing, and the boxes in which to cook the salmon. You
need a safe bay in which to anchor that canoe. If you are to understand the actual life within a specific tribe's territory, you have to
look at the complex of material usage. And rock art of some form,
either pictographs or petroglyphs, will be found in or adjacent to
those complexes in most places on the coast, as well as in areas
of spiritual retreat from the village. Joy Inglis and Hilary Stewart
have identified over ninety petroglyphs on Quadra alone.

I do try to avoid cultural projection, but I confess that during the clam garden searches I wanted someone to have painted the concepts, dreams, and even the fears of those who'd understood the benefit of constructing the walls.

Mink was unhappy. The tide would not go down to the level of his food. He stole Wolf's tail and held it to the fire. Wolf called out: "Hey! Stop that. What do you want?"

Mink hollered, "I want the tide to go down further."

"Okay," says Wolf, "I'll make it go down to the barnacles."

Mink wasn't satisfied and held the tail closer to the fire.

"Okay, okay!" says Wolf. "I'll make it go down to where the cockles grow."

"No way," Mink said, "I want it to go down to the lo xwi we," and he held Wolf's tail right in the middle of the fire.

"Ooh, Owwwh!" howled Wolf, and he made the tide go down to the lowest level of the beach where the lo xwi we was built.

Monday Anchorage clam garden with the Tac on the canoe slide.

7

Abode of Supernatural Beings

John Harper and Mary Morris arranged to meet Bobo and me in the Broughton Archipelago for the 2004 early August low tides. In late July we headed north aboard our old seiner *Adriatic Sea*, towing *Tac*. It was unusually hot when we anchored at Port Harvey in Kwakw_aka_'wakw territory and crossed to the old village on the south side for a swim. Drying off, I walked along the eroded face of the village's kitchen midden and was surprised to see that since my last visit the remains of horizontal and vertical boards had weathered out of packed shell and purple dirt. Directly below lay a black, flaked arrowhead, as if dropped from the midden that day. In a bay southwest of our anchorage, tucked in behind the most exhilarating flare of pictographs on the coast, a wide band of boulders fenced a clam flat in front of another village site.

On August 1 we snugged *Addy* to Windsong Village dock in Echo Bay on Gilford Island. In my old chart book this bay is labelled "Abode of supernatural beings." Their supernatural power may be what is portrayed in the pictographs on the echo-making cliff back of Windsong. According to Kwiksootainuk tales, this territory contains the origin site of the animals of this world, and is the source of the "Dance of the Animals" in which Wolf is the head speaker and, in some stories, Mink is a spy.

After we tied up, John Harper and Billy Proctor both boated around the point from Billy's place across from the Shoal Harbour entrance. A visiting boater offered a huge bowl of prawns to the group gathered at Windsong's picnic table for Billy's tales of the raincoast. Despite the conviviality engendered, we got the next day's schedule organized, and went to bed early enough to rise on August 2 at 5:30 to take advantage of a very low tide.

Harper's plan for the day was to examine the clam garden Billy built over a forty-year period. Billy dug, John mapped, and Mary counted clams per square foot. From this beach Billy harvests approximately thirty clams a week in "R" months all winter. John calculated the garden presently contained 10,000 clams, half of which were a harvestable six to eight centimetres across. Billy carefully reburies undersized clams with their siphon up — in effect spacing and transplanting them as Native gardeners did when digging roots. Because of its constant use, the matrix is well aerated. Since Billy knows when he started and what the production level was when he began, his plot provides some sense of the clam garden process. His small garden's high level of production proves the amount of nutrition attained from accumulative labour is worth the effort and could be the work of a single energetic and observant person.

Billy's wife Yvonne removes siphons and gills from harvested clams since they can hold red tide for some time. However, it's Billy's controversial contention that clams dug from areas only available at *extreme* low tides *and* adjacent to swiftly running water have little chance of ingesting red tide, which he says occurs only in the top fifteen centimetres of the sea. He says local Native people followed these harvesting guidelines in the summers.

Yvonne fries the clams or turns them into chowder or fritters, which they eat approximately three times a week throughout the winter. Butter clams from Broughton beds, dug by both of them during an intense year-long effort, paid for their land.

It was my intention to spend the morning visiting previously unseen clam gardens to compare with those in the south. We took *Tac* back down Cramer Passage, around Steep Island, along Blunden Passage, down Misty Passage and turned into Joe Cove. Extending north into Eden Island, this cove is filled with good-sized clam terraces. Midway up Joe Cove's south side, in behind an island fronting an old village, a deep, walled terrace lies below a snowy shell beach. The water level was a good metre below the top of the terrace walls.

At the head of the cove, a stream exits a small lake that sits between Joe Cove and two anchorages known as Eden Island East and West. Flanking the creek are inward-curved lines of boulders that do look like fish traps. There will, I am sure, soon be many investigations of the relationship between the archeologically accepted fish-trap technology and clam gardens, but an observant person — a pre-contact indigenous harvester, or someone like Billy, minutely tuned to their environment — would notice potential shellfish-nurturing material collecting behind any barrier constructed on a beach.

From Eden Island we crossed Misty Passage to Monday Anchorage, the location of the clam garden Yvonne Maximchuk drew for *Full Moon, Flood Tide*. Our upcoast boating partners Cathy and John Campbell had anchored their *Evening Star I* here the night before to supply us with a good base for exploration. They had helped us scout the bay on a July 27 1.5-metre tide when the inundated beach had revealed only the shadow of an underwater wall that I knew was there. Now the flat beach was laid out in its entirety, with a metre of the wall exposed. Against the bedrock, at the left side, it sloped down to a sandy, 1.25-metre-wide canoe slide. *Tac* slid in. We disembarked and suddenly locked eyes with a small octopus blushing a brilliant, rusty scarlet. It was out of the water on a wall boulder, and after dithering here and there and coiling and uncoiling its many legs in an almost humanly embarrassed manner, it slid into the water and shot like an arrow along and into the wall. Octopi, also known as devilfish, are known to climb out of water to protect eggs or a brood of young, and they feed to a large extent on crabs. It was but one of an even greater variety of creatures we would see on northern, cold-water clam gardens than we had found on the beach down which the ravens strolled.

The clam garden wall appeared to be over one and a half metres tall in some places, and the randomly spurting, soft mud terrace extended far back to boulders below a bedrock rise stuffed with trees. The half-moon-shaped beach had a northern panhandle a quarter of its width deep. The terrace surface was littered with shells of littleneck and butter calms and sported a great variety of colourful starfish. *Piaster brevispinus* starfish are capable of using extendable tube feet at their mouths to ingest clams. The up-beach boulders were covered with clusters of giant thatched barnacles, which rotated their curious Martian heads within high

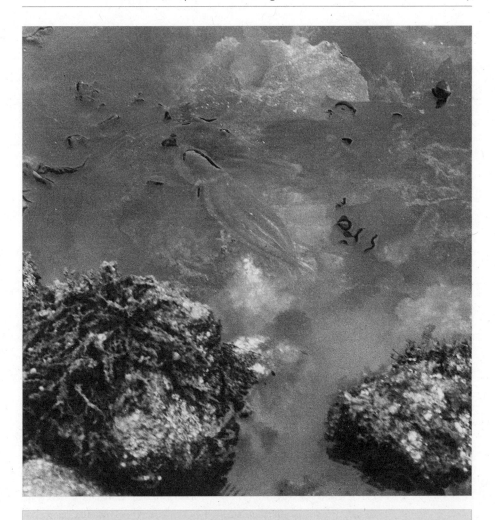

Devilfish seasoned with the flavour of clams

When a woman sees a devilfish in the water on a rock while she is gathering clams, she spears it and puts it into her small clam-digging canoe. When she has many clams, she steams them. Then she puts the devilfish with them when she is about to pour water on the clams. After the water has been poured on, the devilfish is covered over with the clams and it is steamed with the clams that are made into dried clams.[1]

rigid collars. Northern beaches are composed of broken clam shell and the shells of these barnacle.

A torpid mud shrimp lay on the surface near the small, pebble-topped mounds marking the intake to their burrows. During inundation they fan water through these burrows and, like other terrace creatures, help aerate the sand and keep the habitat healthy. We easily extracted cockles from the mud around them. Huge, flaccid purple anemones hung around scattered boulders. A fair-sized Dungeness crab hid under a rock, and the shells of its dismembered relatives lay all over the beach where mink, otters, and raccoons had feasted. Small crabs cleaned up leftovers.

Shorter walls began again beyond a southern rocky point, creating a couple of very narrow ledges. Why were such shallow sections created there, and in places like Old Passage by Insect Island, if larger beds were available? Perhaps they were accessible at different tides as William Scow said, or, as Billy suggests, possessed by different classes of owners.

Cathy discovered a brilliant orange nudibranch on the nearby Tracey Island beach wall and I dug butter clams, littlenecks, and cockles from boot-sucking sand dense with empty butter shells there. Since the mid-beach is the most productive area for clams, and the beach near the wall is least productive, the aim in terracing is to create a larger mid-beach. However, the wall itself harbours a large number of life forms that contribute to, or receive benefit from, the substrate's permeability. If, as marine biologist Ed Ricketts wrote in *Outer Shores*, biology consists entirely of relationships, then this mix of interdependent creatures would have existed in a clam habitat prior to terrace expansion. Interestingly, the beds are less productive when their human cultivator is absent.

The land behind the beach was full of swooping cedar trees, a village site and creek. South was a rock promontory with evidence of camp fires. A shallow pool full of littleneck shells lay against an abrupt rise. Sitting up there on a rock against the cliff, I could view two levels of mirror-flat water — the pond and the sea — each lit differently by the rising sun, and watch clouds drift through different intensities of cerulean. Orange and purple stars seemed to have fallen from the night sky to the white beach below, where they lay amongst green laver clouds. It was intoxicating. Here was fresh water, food, building material, sheltered canoe moorage, and great beauty — the things to sustain life.

I wondered if some terraces might have been constructed in a more calculated way than by simple rock rolling. Had people noticed a small colony of clams growing naturally in a bay, established an outer perimeter by driving wooden stakes such as used in weirs beyond the available beach, rolled the rocks cluttering the surface in behind the stakes, and subsequently aerated and expanded a diminutive habitat by harvesting the clams? Since the beaches *as we know them* are said to have emerged as long as 8,000 years ago, and clams are thought to have appeared over 10,000 years ago, it may be more sensible to return to the scenario in which rocks were just so continuously excavated and piled to the sea end of an existing clam flat that a terrace grew seaward and the hash depth increased over a very long period of harvesting.

We cruised north up Misty Passage to the big midden on Insect Island and strolled along the three levels of the enormous village of Kukwapa that Tsawatainuk Chief Cesaholis claimed in 1914 for clams, hunting, trapping and timber. The Tsawatainuk were given tiny, barren Fly Island just north instead. G'o'g·yewe ("House in the middle") village lies on Baker Island opposite the narrow Old Passage clam terraces. Despite its present designation as a park, a new sign proclaims Kukwapa to be the possession of the Musgamagw, "The Four," a potlatch group consisting of the Kingcome Inlet Tsawatainuk, the Kwicksutainuk, the Haxwa'mis of Wakeman Sound, and the Gwawaenuk of Hikums (Hopetown, on Watson Island).

Kukwapa's sheer size is arresting, but it is only one of many sites in the area whose final date of occupation is unclear. Billy's collection of artifacts from this area ranges from Cascade stone points (the type I saw in Port Harvey, thought to be 4,000 years old) to trade beads and later commercial items. Dr. Don Mitchell, the main archeological surveyor of this entire area, examined the extremely deep midden beneath Billy's house and his huge collection of Broughton artifacts. Mitchell told me that Kukwapa was occupied at three different times and that, at the time Europeans arrived, the Broughtons may have supported 20,000 people — supported them partially, it's now clear, with clams.

Back at Echo Bay, at day's end, we boated around to Proctors' for Harper's PowerPoint clam garden lecture. Yvonne Proctor, Billy, and his co-author Yvonne Maximchuk sat with an upcoast audience, who dug, ate, or sold clams regularly. They focused on John's talk in a different way than the Victoria audience had done. Everyone was fascinated by John's aerial photograph of a 1.5-kilometre-long rock wall and terrace off Valdez Island. It's not yet clear to what degree this technology was used in the Gulf Islands, but the Valdez wall resembles the Broughton structures John recorded from the air.

I raised the question of the necessity of working the gardens. Billy said that in his experience, untended beds were full of dead clams. The hash compacts and clams suffocate. Overproduction, he said, leads to small clams pushing right up to the surface, as is the case on his beach.

The next morning the sky cleared and Billy motored around to sit on *Addy*'s gunnels and engage in his characteristically informative banter. In the past he had marked pictograph sites and anchorages safe in specific winds on my charts; I had found those spots to be exactly where he located them. Now he mentioned that one of the most interesting archeological sites was what might be a fort in a bay just north, and after breakfast we followed his directions to a partially inundated clam garden inside a tidal islet. Islets lend themselves to ideal clam wall configuration since they provide stability for the rock wall and deflect erosion.

Onshore, I struggled through spilling midden up the single, steep, access route onto a semi-detached point of Broughton Island. The entire top was covered by metre-high rectangular mounds outlining where indigenous houses once stood. In the centre was a group of the huge gnarly cedars common to abandoned villages. A fallen log was ablaze with the thick fruiting bodies of Chicken of the Woods fungus, *Polyporus sulphureus* — one side bright orange and the other sulphur yellow. A fringe of trees obscured everything from the water, but there was a lookout from which could be seen all the surrounding waterways. This fortifiable site may have been an outpost of the large village to the south in Deep Harbour, where Chief Dick had dug clams as a child, but it had its own clam resource.

On August 3 we headed down Cramer Passage and turned south around the white beach at Isle Point, which Boas said was called

Dze'g·ade or "having clam digging." We cruised past the recently surveyed clam gardens at the north end of Bonwick Island, which Johnny Scow had claimed in its entirety for clams in 1914. The clam stations he and Chief Mountain claimed, almost none of which were given as reserve land, appear to be have been used for an immense amount of time by the local people. I hope that now the existence, usage, and antiquity of these stations are known, the local people will never be denied access to this resource by government agencies "protecting" it from their use or licensing it to outsiders. These living artifacts, as Billy has demonstrated, thrive on sensitive *domestic* use.

As we headed south through Spring Passage, a vast humpback lazed along the *Adriatic Sea*'s starboard side, crossed and swam straight in front for a while, then swung to port to circle a cluster of rocks. We spent the night in Village Anchorage and next morning slid *Tac* between scarves of mist to Mimkum-lese, on the west side of Village Island, where the low tide had unrolled a slick of boulder-dotted, sulphurous mud. One would have to work to get it, but there had been food everywhere in the area, and the beach in front of this village of the Mamalilikulla people was a tribute to a fecundity that produced era after era of occupation. Above the beach rose a six-metre bank of butter-clam-shell-studded dark soil; below, a white crushed-shell strand, punctuated with glass and pottery fragments, stretched to the mud in which the Orange Crush bottles of my childhood, metal parts from fish boats, and remnants of gas washing machines made a visual bridge to the burial islands. Somewhere there, beyond the modern cement bone containers, lies the mossy flathead skull I saw during our first trip here in 1989 when the last totem pole still stood.

What that person ate would be instructive, as the clam gardens around Village Island appeared smaller in scope than those just to the north. In the vast maze of islands, between Harbledown

> On May 20, 1792, Captain George Vancouver visited village huts in Puget Sound.
>
> *In them were hung up to be cured by the smoke of the fire they kept constantly burning, clams, mussels, and a few other kinds of fish, seemingly intended for their winter's sustenance. The clams perhaps were not all reserved for that purpose, as we frequently saw them strung and worn about the neck, which, as inclination directed, were eaten, two, three, or half a dozen at a time.[2]*

Island, Blackfish Sound, Queen Charlotte Strait and the mainland, that we had been exploring, we had found both sloping mud
clam flats and constructed rock-walled clam terraces. What had
been utilized and what built depended on what marine conditions
and geography allowed, but the degree of cultivation needed was
also related to individual tribal ownership of salmon and oolichan
streams up Kingcome Inlet, Thompson and Bond Sounds and
of the fish-bearing rivers up Knight Inlet directly east of Village
Island. Fishing rights along waterways were specifically appor-
tioned to different tribes and not always equally. Some Mamalilikulla leased the Tzatsisnukomi village site to Knight Inlet people
sometime in the early 1890s so Village Island people could have
oolichan rights at the head of Knight. The Mamalilikulla gained
oolichan rights, and the Knight Inlet group gained a location
outside the long, isolating inlet in which, however, they continued to own huge salmon runs. Not every family or tribe needed
the quantity of clams that had motivated the construction of the
Broughton clam gardens.

8

Gathering at the End of the Road

Boating to Kanish Bay on the west side of Quadra Island from Waiatt involves running north across the western end of Hole in the Wall rapids, through the Upper and Lower Okisollo rapids at the top of Quadra, and turning south at Granite Point. Pictographs painted near the point were first recorded in a drawing by archeologist Dr. Don Mitchell in 1967. There are two face forms and possibly a salmon entering a weir near a canoe with an upright figure, but most red marks are difficult to interpret. Farther into Kanish Bay is a more obvious, new, white pictogram of a huge figure stretching out cartoon arms to a wild face sporting a Mick Jagger-ish red tongue that I hope is not all that remains of an overpainted Native pictograph. Large letters declare "Kilroy was Here!"

Entering Kanish Bay proper, a boater passes an open grassy village site and the neck of Small Inlet, where the path allowed residents to move between Waiatt and Kanish without a lengthy paddle. Portside, past an oyster farm, are the good anchorages behind the Chained Islands where we'd anchored *Addy* on our way home from the Broughton.

Today it's possible to drive to Granite Bay from Quathiaski Cove. After the pavement ends, the gravel road crosses a creek and terminates at a ramshackle dock. At the base of a rudimentary ramp, Red's Snack Shack firmly announces it's closed, even though it is largely open to the elements. A barbecue rusts at the end of a float so askew that flowers in boxes, growing straight skyward, accentuate its remarkable tilt.

On August 27, 2004, the same Dr. Mitchell who had surveyed in the Broughton and here in Kanish Bay in the 1960s strolled down the ramp. Now retired from the University of Victoria, Don is a leading expert on coastal archeology. He was joining the gathering, organized by John Harper, of folks interested in looking for clam gardens here in Kanish Bay and validating the existence of clam garden technology. Tucked under Don's arm were his original site notes for Kanish. We waited on the dock until John and Mary Morris arrived from Waiatt Bay, where they had gone for their first look at that extensive clam garden complex. After helping dock the *Lizzie M*, the four of us exchanged notes and theories. Don lent a benevolent ear to John's and my speculations. We were sure. Don, the cool professional, would see.

Cameraman Aaron Szimanski and producer Diane Wood arrived to check the next day's expedition schedule. They had both travelled with John in the Broughton in 2003, shooting footage for David J. Woods Production's *Ancient Sea Gardens*. Diane asked why I thought the Archeology Branch had been so indifferent to information I'd sent them in the 1990s. I had no clear answer, but said I continued to be puzzled why clam terraces had never previously been reported. Don interjected, explaining the distinction between two different kinds of education archeologists may receive that he felt might be relevant. Some schools, he said, emphasize the broad ethnographic, linguistic, geographical, and anthropological components of archeological education that Boas recommended. Others provide a more technological training, which could produce graduates with limited bureaucratic and custodial attitudes. I added that a lack of both governmental funding and legal support for prosecuting archeological site abusers might lead government archeologists to neglect thoughtful new exploration and analysis in order to undertake the salvage operations vandalism and new development cause.

Those participating in the expedition planned to spend the night on Quadra to facilitate a 7 a.m. start so they could work through the next day's 8:30 low tide. Mary and I drove south to the Lekwiltok Band's Tsa-Kwa-Luten Lodge, which stands near the village of Salish speakers that Captain Vancouver visited in 1792. We had dinner with ethnobotonist Dr. Nancy Turner, a highly regarded authority on indigenous peoples' plants, foods,

and their preparation, Chief Kim Recalma-Clutesi of the Qualicum Nation, Chief Adam Dick, and Mary's mother Dee Morris,
all of whom were staying at the lodge.

I repeated to Nancy the question Diane had asked about archeologists' and anthropologists' earlier lack of interest in clam gardens. Nancy said that clams were dug by women and children,
and early archeologists were mainly men, more interested in the
hunting, fishing, and masculine ritual lore. Nancy related how
a Native friend had explained that, when she was a child, butter clams were pit cooked, as fern roots were, then shelled and
woven into ropes and strung on sticks from the ocean spray shrub
(*Holodiscus discolor*). When her friend's family went south to pick
hops, they took smoked and dried clams to sell to Tacoma Native
people, who loved them and slung the strings around their necks
so they could pull clusters off for snacks. Nancy said one of the
attractions of clams was their storability, which made them not
only important feast food but also tradable. It was surely such clam
strings that were offered to Valdes as a treat and that Vancouver
observed hanging in huts of Puget Sound villages.

Mary and I returned to Granite Bay to sleep on *Lizzie*. The light

*Kanish Bay
— island and
white clam
shell midden,
August 2004.*

burned late in Don's truck as he studied his old notes. Next morning, heavy rain had drenched the fir-padded slopes of the bay. The shell midden spilling from a grassy knob west of the creek, and Don's recollections of a post office and hotel that were still visible nearby in the 1960s, gave a sense of early Native habitation and the 500 people reported to have lived here in the 1930s. Now a few hand-built houses were tucked in the woods, and a very occasional car motor broke the silence. *Lizzie M*'s passengers struggled down the almost vertical ramp as the tide ebbed north and drained the bay. A rank, gassy smell rose from sticky mud off the mouth of the creek as an immaculate pair of snow geese paddled ashore. The still water of the bay doubled every form.

Linda Hogarth of the Campbell River Museum arrived with her husband Chris, and they launched their canoe to join the day's hunt. Linda and her son Ryan had paddled the bay at a June low tide, mapped eleven clam terraces, and set the stage for this expedition. *Lizzie M* set sail as one, two, three, then many clam terraces rose out of the sea to be counted, photographed, and discussed. Herons stood thoughtfully on the rock walls, and two raccoons scrambled away from their low-tide buffet.

We deposited Aaron, with his camera, on a rocky weed-cushioned lump off a curiously elegant island at the northeast exit of Granite Bay. He intended to film the tide later as it rose over the clam garden between that island and the main body of Quadra.

Kanish Bay clam terrace.
PHOTO
BY LINDA
HOGARTH

A faintly indented trail flowed like smoke up the island's burnt-gold moss to dolmen-like boulders against a backdrop of trees. It seemed a set for an ancient drama.

Mary ferried Don and Nancy to join Linda on the opposite shore's terrace as *Lizzie M* drifted motionless mid-channel. Later, when I joined Don on the terrace, I asked, "Well?"

He smiled. "I'm convinced."

It was a gratifying moment. However, to my eye this and other clearly walled terraces in Kanish Bay were rather heavily sprinkled with small barnacled stones. John referred to it as a "veneer of cobble," and its origin was unknown to him. Any clam digger would find these a continuing nuisance and toss them aside. If earlier cobbles had been discarded, had these risen over time or washed onto the surface from the steep hillside above? With their cobble veneer, the Kanish terraces gave far less evidence of recent clamming than did the clearer surfaces in Waiatt. According to Robert Galois, the gazetteer who tracked the movement of the coast's Kwakwalla speakers, Weewiakay Chief Harry Assu said Kanish had been a herring station. Perhaps these terraces, like those at Shoal Harbour, were always multi-use and long abandoned as seriously cultivated gardens.

Don, John, Linda, and I headed out in the runabout *Kingfisher* to see what else the bay might reveal. John excitedly counted at least twenty-two clam gardens. Big, little, deep, shallow — they'd been built everywhere that made sense to us and in some places it didn't. A particularly interesting complex at the entrance to Small Inlet had a naturally sloped clam flat flanked by long, narrow, walled terraces. A low pass from there through into an outer bay revealed more terraces. Why make the effort to flank a large clam bed with more beds? It might be that butter clams raised on the less mucky, built-up beds are superior in taste or substance. There was much about growth conditions, as well as the pressure of population, ownership, rights, privileges, access, enterprise, and trade, that marine biologists and social scientists would want to investigate in locations like Waiatt and Kanish that contain extensive construction.

John headed *Kingfisher* to the village site north of Small Inlet where, above a clam terrace, a layer of white shell and a golden, grassy flat rose towards a creek. Just south, in a baylet, Don pointed to two canoe slides across a cobble-laden beach. He said logs on which the canoes slid would have been laid across the clearings and anchored with boulders. Joy Inglis told me petroglyph boulders, like those near the Seawolf petroglyph at the south end of Quadra, often anchored the top logs.

Onshore, Don was interested to discover more house forms than he'd noticed in the 1960s, what he thought was a ploughed area, and two burial cairns on the slope behind. He startled me by estimating the cairns dated from the extremely early period, *circa* AD 1200. Don said they were part of an ancient Salish village site here, occupied by the Lekwiltok post-contact and more recently by a white homestead. He added that in pre-contact times, the Salish linguistic group, which extended far south into the Columbia Plateau, also occupied territory as far north in Johnstone Strait as Port Neville. There, at the trenched fortress at Robber's Knob, above splendid petroglyphs, an odd but finely worked stone *whatsit* was found, far north of similar ones discovered in the Salish Gulf Islands that are thought to be 2,500 years old.

As we left the site, Nancy remarked on the dearth of Native people's food plants, like high bank clover and silverweed, but she carried away the nettle stalks common to villages. Onboard, we watched her break open the stalks to release the fibre that women twisted into the twine men used to make fishing nets.

I raised my eyes to see two harbour porpoises break the silver skin of the sea just beyond the boat, set loose a wavelet that skimmed straight across the bay, and disappear. Most of the clam gardens had remained out of that remarkably still water for four hours. We were at the south end of the northern tidal flow, and while slack water might last only five minutes at the Nawatko Rapids in Seymour Inlet, it lingered much longer here.

As the rain intensified, we collected Aaron from his rock, and the crew downed salmon sandwiches made from Kim's newly canned sockeye. To facilitate filming, John used *Kingfisher* to slowly tow *Lizzie* past the old village. Sworn to motionless silence, we listened as Aaron filmed Don on the back deck. Fully conscious of the importance of what he was saying, Don carefully stated that, as a young archeologist in the 1960s, he'd seen the terraces but had not understood their function. He said he was now convinced they were clam gardens constructed by Native inhabitants for the production of clams. They may have been overlooked, he added, because they appear, so far, to be without precedent in the world.

At Diane's request I spoke to the camera of Keekus's directing my attention to the Waiatt Bay clam complex and of my appreciation for the opening she had provided me to a new vision of indigenous Northwest culture. I emphasized that my first look at the clam terraces convinced me that what she'd said of their construction and use made sense. As I turned away from the camera, I saw the Kanish terraces had slid beneath the risen sea, away from our sight and theorizing, to remain much of the time an unseen wonder tended by the sea and its creatures. The rain occluded the sea's surface and the flooding tide engraved it with a filigree of watery rhythms through which we floated back to the end of the road.

Bill Reid's Raven and the First Men. *The men are emerging from a butter clam shell.* PHOTO BY W. MCLENNAN, UBC MUSEUM OF ANTHROPOLOGY.

There is a story they tell in the Queen Charlotte Islands of Raven creating the first people. After the great flood, the sea ebbed away from Rose Spit at the north end of Haida Gwaii, and Raven stalked along the great expanse of sand, gorging on stranded delicacies. For once he had enough to eat. But Raven, being Raven, decided other appetites — his curiosity and the itch to meddle and provoke things, to play tricks on the world and its creatures — remained unsatisfied. He gazed up and down the beach and sighed. He crossed his wings behind him and strutted along the sand with his head cocked and his eyes and ears alert for any unusual sight or sound. The mountains, the sky ablaze with sun, the moon and the stars were all where he'd placed them. To be sure, Raven grumbled, it was very pretty, but it was lifeless. He let out a loud exasperated S C R O A A K !

Before the echo of his cry faded, he heard a muffled squeak. Raven looked up and down the beach. Nothing. He strutted back and forth. Still nothing. Suddenly he spied the white flash of a giant clam shell half buried in the sand, and as his shadow fell across it he heard another squeak. Peering down into the opening between the halves of the shell, he saw it was full of tiny creatures cowering in fear.

Raven was delighted! Here was a break in the monotony of the day. But how was he to get the creatures to come out and play? He leaned his head close to the shell opening and with all the cunning of his trickster tongue he coaxed and cajoled the little beings to come out and play in his shiny new world. Raven has two voices; one is harsh and strident, and the other, which he used on the pale little things, is a seductive, bell-like croon that seems to come from the depth of the sea. First one, then another of the shell dwellers emerged. They scurried back when they saw Raven, but eventually curiosity overcame their caution and all scrambled out. Very strange creatures they were. Two legged like Raven, but without fur, feathers, or great beak; their skin naked except for black hair around flat-featured heads. Instead of the strong wings of Raven, the first humans had stick-like arms that waved and fluttered about.

Raven amused himself with the little beings for some time, but soon he began to get bored. These creatures were so helpless out in the world. They needed shelter from the sun and rain. There were no girls! Somewhere, Raven thought, there must be girls. As he began to search under logs and behind boulders, the tide went out, and as it reached its lowest level, Raven spotted giant chitons clinging to rocks. Their single shell was fastened tightly to the stone,

and huge soft lips flowed around their edges. He pried one off with his beak and inside was a girl. He pried off another, and another, and in each was a girl. They were like the creatures he'd found in the clam shell but softer and rounder. He gathered the chiton girls up on his back and brought them to the clam boys. Some say Raven flung the chiton girls at the private parts of the boys, and their close adherence caused strange new feelings in the bodies of the clam creatures and this led to the creation of the first people. Others tell the tale more politely, but since that day Raven has never been bored. From the pairing of the strong muscles of the clam and the soft lips of the chitons came the boys and girls of the first families. These new humans were not timid shell dwellers but strong children of the wild stormy shores between the land and the sea.[1]

9

'We can't count the years . . .'

In August 2005 I woke up, anchored in Port Harvey, and glanced to shore where, the previous night, pilchards, absent from this coast for fifty years, had flung themselves up out of a dark sea like lit bulbs. Now the ebbing tide revealed a hash-filled boulder terrace on what, at a higher tide, had seemed an unremarkable shore. Thirty metres away was a minor addition to the lengthening list of cultivated clam habitats scrolled against coastal shores. It was possible to find clam terraces anywhere practical now that their configuration was meaningful. John Harper reported seeing a clam garden at Brentwood Bay on Vancouver Island and a number near Sitka, Alaska, when he was mapping from the air there this summer. Carl Humchitt, a Heiltsuk fisherman and GPS engineer, told me there were extremely productive old clam beds in some bays in their territory that had needed to be shored up, which suggested they had been artificially constructed.

The extent of Native mariculture was realigning concepts of indigenous economy and our understanding of the trajectory of indigenous cultural development. The fact that it had been neglected for so long exposed the cultural and gender bias that had obscured its importance. Soon it might be possible to date the advent of this technology, and this would help clarify which indigenous tribes had constructed the clam gardens. At the very end of the film *Ancient Sea Gardens: Mystery of the Pacific Northwest*, a voiceover claims carbon dating of an Echo Bay midden indicates the shift to major butter clam consumption occurred there 2,000 years ago.[1]

Finding a clam garden in Port Harvey was really no surprise. During trips through this territory I had become familiar with the many village sites and middens, and the variety of pictographs ablaze in granite alcoves that indicated long First Nations engagement with this area. But a trip to more northern territory had extended my list of clam garden locations. Two weeks earlier I'd climbed down into *Tac* from the *Adriatic Sea* to scout islands in Codville Lagoon on King Island, where Dean and Burke channels head east to Bella Coola. Codville's entrance is directly across Fisher Channel from Lama Passage, a route west to the offshore cluster of islands around Bella Bella that are occupied by the Heiltsuk.

It's wise to enter the shallow, narrow neck of the lagoon with some care, but, once inside, one is rewarded with the sight of a line of red rings painted on the Codville Island cliff. Below the painting is an exquisite ledge, where a mat of crisp, heart-shaped leaves surrounds a stone bench. The ledge faces a baylet providing access to a trail up to Sagar Lake. As the trail rises to the lake, the soil, the plants, and finally the sand in the lake take on intensifying red tones. When I waded in the lake, my legs appeared red, reminding me of the honoured role ruddy tones play in this

Codville Lagoon clam garden, 2005.

indigenous culture: the red ochre of pictographs, red salmon, red cedar bark worn at certain ceremonials, the red snapper whose colour evaporates as it dies, and the valued blaze of copper. King Island itself is a source of red pigment and north, at Port John, the closest large village site, is the largest collection of red pictographs anywhere on the coast.

East of Codville Island lie clustered islets, between which the ebbing tide drains a series of flats. On the north side of the most westerly islet of this group there is a small wall extending to the next island, and the bridge area is full of clam hash. Although bedrock protrusions in the next bay north of that islet had been joined to create a small terrace, I could see nothing at this tide on the scale of the Waiatt Bay complex. But I was excited that the presence of the essential concept of clam garden technology indicated a practice in common with that of more southern tribes.

Carl Humchitt told me that this territory contains a huge diversity of food material and that harvesting seasons overlap more than they do down south. But clams are important. He emphasized that shellfish beds near a village had not generally been used until they were needed by "the Grannies and Aunties" left behind when hunting and food gathering took villagers away for long periods. Before the villagers left, they brought in more clams and urchins, which were stowed on those nearby clam terraces to add to what the Grannies could harvest. He added that mussel- or giant barnacle-bearing rocks were sometimes moved into convenient locations, and over-harvested clam beds were reseeded with full-size and "button" butter clams as well as littlenecks and now Manilas. In this area, crucial food sources were managed by stewards. If there was a report of a low return, the area was left fallow for a long time.

Encounters with such pockets of indigenous industry, near pictographs, fish traps, and deep midden, always created in me an overwhelming feeling of a settled presence in place that Carl's stories evoked. I was fascinated by evidence of lives adapted to a landscape's essential features, and some of those features adapted to enhance life. I was certainly amused by the way a culture can develop, buoyed up by the humblest of contributing elements — in the case of clams, one so embedded and humble no one appeared to have thought to analyze its role.

I remained awed by the harmonious simplicity of the stone-walled terraces and equally by the impossibility of separating any activity within such a culture from its whole environment — a unity some find elusive in contemporary life. Red is a colour to us, but red would be meaningful in a different way when you acknowledged many of your necessities come in shades of blood.

Earlier that summer, south in Sliammon/Klahoose territory, Anne Dewar handed me a red slab of frozen salmon at the Cortes Island Friday Market and commented on the clam gardens Billy Proctor had described to her in the Broughton. She said when her family moved to Harlequin House in Gorge Harbour on Cortes in 1960, they'd been intrigued by a long, east-to-west-oriented boulder wall below their house, which faced the harbour entrance. The house was named after the Harlequin ducks that frequented the deep flat behind the wall. The flat was then so covered with upstanding oysters that it created a white background over which, at high tide, they could look down from the house to see the ducks swimming. The house, which was set atop the site of a Native village thought to have been abandoned before 1900, looked out the narrow harbour entrance from the precise angle at which the Guide Islands outside did not block the view straight south. Another Cortesian, Vicky de Bore, recalled walls she had seen when they surveyed for dock piers near the new home now built atop the Harlequin House site.

Such tantalizing information suggested I dedicate one of May's three low tides to a Cortes expedition. As the tide ebbed at 11:40 a.m. on May 24, I walked past the hydro box threading power to Tan Island in the middle of Gorge Harbour, and onto a grassy bluff. Creamy patches of clam hash lay within a series of rock boundaries stretching west to a tidal island. A clearly defined, gently

Gorge Harbour clam terrace, May 2005.

canted, 1.5-kilometre-long wall snaked from the new pier west to tidal islets and continued northwest to the government dock. It bore an amazing resemblance to the long walls in John's aerial photos from the Broughton. This wall varied in height from roughly one to two metres and was exposed almost to its base when the tide dropped to 0.2 metres at 12:30. The amount of work that would have been required to construct the wall, and the length of time needed to build up the level surface, was astounding.

Red sunstars curled among boulders similar in size to those forming other walls, but there was less vegetation and fewer critters than at Waiatt Bay. Submerged at the foot of the wall was an indeterminable depth of pale sand. Beyond a point where the terrace turned northwest, the beach was flat and walled but not as groomed as the eastern section. This may be the result of shellfish culture, as an oyster lease now occupies the central portion of the terrace. Boulders had been removed from part of the flat in the 1950s to drive a logging truck along the beach.

The wall and terrace have an instructive relationship to the oyster industry in France that may have affected its structure, but which also indicates the marine fertility that must have motivated indigenous wall construction in the Gorge. After disease nearly wiped out the French oyster beds in 1968-69, French farmers studied the quality of oysters from all over the world to find a source to revitalize their industry. The Gorge Pacific oysters (*Crassotrea gigas* or Japanese oyster), considered the finest available, were loaded on planes and shipped to France, where they flourished. Norm Gibbons, who pioneered mariculture at Refuge Cove in the 1980s, explained that Gorge oysters were exceptionally prolific and tasty due to three factors that have been much studied by various interested government agencies. First, the Gorge waters are considered the most ideal shellfish-growing conditions on the coast because they are extremely rich in nutrients. Second, strong currents flood directly into the wall area and swirl east and around the bay before exiting. Third, studies indicate a fairly high salinity level of 27 to 28 parts per thousand, which is better than Refuge's 22 parts per thousand and just below the open ocean's 33 parts per thousand.

Norm thought the oysters Anne saw in the 1960s would likely have built up after a series of oyster "general spat falls" that occurred in 1943, 1956, and 1966, during which the entire coast would be covered with infant oysters. These "spat falls" tended to run in ten- to fifteen-year cycles, but by the 1980s they had failed several times, which led to the development of artificial oyster culture. After a "spat fall," oysters could build up on top of each other to a depth of one metre, and they were harvested for years. Norm thinks it unlikely the main area of the Gorge Harbour wall underwent major modifications before the 1980s, although its use as a bagged shellfish storage area could have compacted the surface.

The walled terrace was ideally placed for maximum nutrient deposit for butter clam culture. Waiatt Bay receives different and cooler seas, but, interestingly, nutrients there would be funnelled directly through its heavily terraced northern entrance and across to the long walls on its south side.

The deepest section of the Gorge terrace was north and west of the largest tidal island, where the distance inland from the wall was at least eighteen metres. This remarkably level area was covered with live oysters and oyster culture debris as well as Manila, littleneck, razor, mahogany, and butter clam shells. There was a fair amount of barnacle growth on small cobble.

Midden spilling out from under trees onshore suggested lengthy indigenous use of the Gorge, which is known to the Sliammon as Yip'iikww ("Break the ice") and Sa'yilh ("Two waters in one"). The cliff rising abruptly on the west side of the single entrance bears both image and tally-mark pictographs. Anne recalls a spiral trail to the top from which, local legend insists, boulders were dropped on intruding canoes. Anne's father, Dunc Robertson, used to tell how, during fog, a Native girl would be left on the Guide Islets to sing returning canoes into the entrance, which is why the islets are so named. Although gulf seas flush the bay, heavy wave action is blocked by these islets and by Marina Island.

The Gorge is presently an overdeveloped, and controversial, commercial shellfish enclave. It would be interesting to discover what effect this has on the clam terrace. Although its origins are not understood by those who use it, it is in an oyster grower's interest to maintain the wall. But it should also be given protected status.

When I returned to my boat at Squirrel Cove, a few Klahoose folk were on the dock, waiting for the clam buyer with sacks of clams from Prideaux Haven across on the east shore of Desolation

Sound. Low tides coincide, of course, with the federal fisheries department's regulated commercial clam openings, which still provide local Native people with a cash crop from ancient beds.

On May 26 I crossed Desolation to Prideaux Haven Marine Park (Qu kwamen, meaning "The right side") and slid *Tac* into a bay where a wide, 2.5-metre-high boulder berm connects Eveleigh Island to the mainland. The rock pile resembles something shoved into place by the edge of a glacier rather than anything that humans could make without major earthmoving equipment. The berm's centre is crossed by a canoe slide bordered by oysters and an uncountable number of small mussels. On the inner northeast flank, hash-filled pockets like those at Stopford Point have been built, and a little lower, on the mainland side of the berm, a half-moon of beach was cleared down to datum, creating an oyster-free clam bed. My shellfish-growing companion Scott Remple climbed back into the boat exclaiming about the "remarkably appropriate engineering."

We motored north around Eveleigh Island, into Prideaux Haven proper and drifted into Copplestone Island Passage at the bottom of the 0.2-metre tide. Two spectacularly balanced, Volkswagen-sized boulders mark the entrance to a 1.5-kilometre-long basin on the mainland side. At this tide, a seventy-five-centimetre waterfall flowed out from the basin over a long, rounded outcrop that forms an almost complete barrier. North of the waterfall, rocks had been piled to beef up a lower spot of bedrock through which

Flea Village clam flat, 2005.

threaded a trickle of water. The outcrop meant the hidden basin, essentially a lagoon, had no need for a wall. It was mainly clear of loose boulders, although the occasional rock tip protruded. Since it is near such rocks that clam diggers say to dig for butters, Delia Becker, my second shellfish-growing advisor, applied fork to sand and dug up a cockle, Manila and littleneck clams, and, twenty-five centimetres down, empty butter clam shells. Scat-tered around the basin were a number of false jingle shells, the holed lower carapace of a mem-ber of the family *Anomiidae*, also known as the native rock oysters. Like native Olympic oysters that were once more prolific, they favour lagoon-type conditions.

Fish-trap forms:

Stone fish trap.

Outside the basin, leather stars, tiny flounders, and large spider crabs worked around a 10.5-metre-long, heart-shaped stone form in one metre of water. The shape was so precise it declared itself a human-engineered structure dedicated to a specific use, and the perfection of its preservation sent shivers up my spine. The depth of water confounded evaluation of how much of the stone form's depth might be buried in the loose silt of the bottom. Heart-shaped fish traps, built by Tlingit people, exist in Alaska, where they're accompanied by similarly shaped petroglyph carv-ings. Across the passage on Copplestone Island was a tiny, walled pocket beach, and to the north a huge, three-lobed clam flat almost divided the island in two.

Stake outline.

Stone outline.

We let the current drift us south over the graceful stone form. Given its coverage at this low tide, I could not imagine it ever emerging from the water. Perhaps a basketry fence had been anchored on top. South, in Tenedos Bay, the drainage from Upper and Lower Unwin lakes had previously harboured coho salmon and cutthroat trout. Fish traps were built in areas where fish natu-rally rested between tides, as well as near stream mouths, and Cop-plestone Passage, blocked at its north end at low tide, might be a useful area into which to drive fish. What we were seeing amongst this cluster of islands on the east side of Desolation Sound was a food complex that nurtured a number of species, of which clams were one important element. The outer islands deflected the pre-vailing wind, and within the clustered islands only minimal wall-ing was needed.

We headed north and in behind Roffey Island. In 1792, Archibald

*Sliammon
Village multi-
use rock works,
September
2005.*

Menzies wrote he had climbed up to a fortified mound he named
Flea Village. He noted that planks had been stuck out from cracks
to foil attackers. Even now the only access is via a defendable
maple tree at the back. A strong stream flows along the site's south
side. In 1862, Robert Homfray met a group of Native people at
Yechoosen ("Starting to go up Toba"), north of the fort, in what is
now called Homfray Channel, paddling two canoes stacked with
dried salmon.

We brought *Tac* right up to a semicircular line of rocks fronting
a clam flat below the fort site. There is said to be a canoe slide on
the north side, although since Francis Barrow reported "Saulter
and Frank" were building a fish boat there in the late 1930s, I
suspect there has been considerable modification. Two bays to
the northwest have small cleared beaches and canoe slides, and
archeological site reports indicate a fish trap to the south. At high
tide one can slip south past Copplestone Point into Laura Cove,
slide into Copplestone Passage, cross Prideaux Haven and the
Eveleigh Island canoe slide, and head out via Otter Pass. It's a
short paddle in behind bird-nesting rocks to Tenedos Bay, where
in 1792 Archibald Menzies recorded seeing an enormous bank of
fish-drying racks.

South, at the north bay of Portage Cove, a clam flat had been
groomed around and behind a tidal island. The midden depth
through the portage attests to the length of time the route from
Prideaux Haven and Tenedos Bay into Wooten Bay, to the The-

odosia's salmon resource, has been used. Sliammon/Klahoose
people could move from Malaspina to Flea Village sheltered from
uncomfortable seas or unfriendly eyes.

On September 1, at the invitation of ex-fisherman and logger
Norm Gallagher, the Sliammon field recognizance officer and
advisor to the Sliammon Treaty Society, I visited the Sliammon
village T'eshusm to view boulder structures the band considers
multi-use rock works. As the tide ebbed to a 3.9 low, I tied *Tac*
to the dock below the band-owned Lund Hotel. Norm drove me
south to the "Rez" above Powell River, crossed a bridge above the
Sliammon Creek salmon hatchery, turned off the highway, and
parked northwest of the old Catholic church, where a reef pointed
to Harwood Island.

Norm's arm traced a swoop of boulders arcing forty-five metres
west from the sand swath below his truck. "Fish traps. For herring.
And I've seen salmon stuck in them. Cedar branches were laid out
here for the herring to spawn on. My grandmother used to take
me down here to dig butters and littlenecks when I was little."
He pointed at one of the half-buried boulders within the outlines.
"She'd sit and crack open a clam, eat it raw. Gave me one but I
couldn't eat it, choked. She said I was fussy. The clams were made
into soup and some she strung onto sticks and dried. Ate them
all the time." He turned back towards the sand and added that
in those years it would have been filled in the spring with racks
covered with roe-laden branches off which he'd pluck handfuls
to eat. Trapped salmon would have been heading up Sliammon
Creek in the fall.

Norm led me along the thirty-centimetre-high boulder line to
where it joined a second ongoing swoop containing an occasional,
and deliberate, kink. At that slightly higher elevation I began to see
both straight and curved boulder lines creating a giant stone net
that covered the entire point down to the water. Both the length
and height of the walls varied, but many runs of boulders were
from thirty to ninety centimetres in height and contained areas
from twenty-five to ninety metres square. Smaller, oval hoops of
stone near the shore had cleared sandy bottoms. A taller line of
boulders appeared to come straight inland from the most westerly
finger of the point and made a breakwater from the north.

Norm's Salish name for the walls was *wuxwuthin*. I asked if

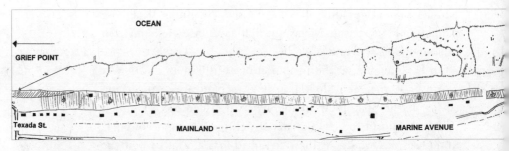

Sliammon rock that word defined the wall or the process, and after some thought
enclosures. he said it meant the process of building. Chief William Mitch-
Adapted from ell had likened the word's meaning to the breakwater at Powell
base map River, which is freestanding. The word does not seem to refer, as
by Dayton *lo xwi we* may, to the bottom of the tide. A Nu-chah-nulth term,
and Knight, *t'i`mi`q*, refers to a clam beach where rocks were "removed or
Consulting thrown aside."[2]
Engineers

Within the Sliammon rock barriers were small barnacle-dotted
cobbles, littleneck and horse clam shells, the occasional jingle
shell, and, in lower areas, slicks of green sea lettuce. Pacific oysters had colonized some spots. There was still food to be found,
but when I raised my eyes from the shore I looked straight at the
striped stack of the Powell River Paper Mill. The mill was built
in 1910 after a dam was constructed above the falls, below which
Native people had caught the salmon that spawned in Powell
Lake. Old-timer Curly Woodward, writing in *Mysterious Powell
Lake*, says that when he was a child, for several years he watched
Native people catching salmon that were attempting to enter the
system, but the runs died out. When the dam was raised again in
1924, it flooded the Theodosia drainage and destroyed that run.
Major elements of this food complex are either extinct or too con-
taminated by effluent and sewage for harvesting.

Norm suggested we drive through Powell River and Westview
to Grief Point (Xa'kww7em). South of a lookout adorned with
new totem poles on Marine Avenue, opposite the northern tip of
Texada Island, he had me look down over a beach of cleared sand,
rock enclosures, and canoe slides. One straight, sand-filled slide, at
least forty-five metres from sea to shore, gave a sense of the depth
of the beach. Scattered along the surface of the strand, and out to
a shore-parallelling mass of boulders creating a consistent seaside

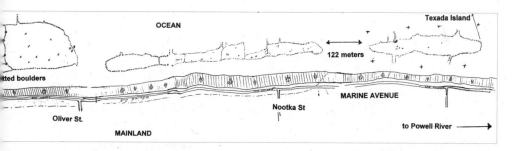

barrier and a level beach, was a bewildering number of rock lines, arcs, and pen-creating arrangements of boulders.

The length and depth of the beach below us resembled John's photo of the Valdez Island clam structure, but this strand stretches close to three kilometres. If these were fish traps, they would also support clam growth. On Grief Point itself are multiple-use stone traps like those at Sliammon. A note in an archeological site report says Dr. Marlett, an old-time resident, reported there were rock walls standing one and a quarter metres tall here in the 1920s. It reminded me that Norm Gibbons had said when massive deposits of native Olympic oysters were all but wiped out in Washington State, growers made unsuccessful attempts to cultivate them commercially in stone pens. When the city of Powell River began building a public beach walk here, Norm Gallagher located pitted boulders behind one of the largest stone enclosures which contains two canoe slides and three slides/traps/entrances open to the sea. He also photographed six petroglyph boulders on the beach north of the rock enclosures.

Norm looked thoughtfully down. "How long?" he said. "We can't count the years it took to build — the number of people."

The stream that had entered the village there was dammed to provide water for the town of Powell River, and the sockeye died out. When reserves were instituted, the band was confined to the Sliammon reserve north of town. Norm spoke with feeling about the reserve process that separated the Sliammon/Klahoose/Homalco group, which spoke *ey7a7juuthem* ("Talk the language"), into discrete units. "If you look at the family trees, we are one," he said. He felt the Island Comox, although a related Salish people, do not hold such a close relationship to them and "do not speak the same language. The Salish," Norm said, "are an enormous group." He was careful to refer to the Waiatt Bay territory as belonging to Salish-speaking people, but diplomatically sidestepped issues of ownership.

Back at the Sliammon Treaty Society office, bookkeeper June Williams, Susan Pielle's granddaughter, pulled out an old photo of branches of herring spawn on racks. In front of the racks, a small boy, as Norm would have been, crammed a fistful of roe into his mouth. The people here, as at Shoal Harbour and Kanish Bay, had used rock constructions in which clams grew to collect herring roe. Maybe clams grew where stone herring traps were built.

June also showed me a picture of the very beautiful Jeannie Dominic barbequing butterflied salmon over an open fire in the 1950s. I was struck by how abrupt a cultural shift the Sliammon had undergone with the loss of superior food resources like clam beds and the salmon, herring and roe.

The office hall was lined with a series of maps showing aspects of Sliammon land claims. The territory — "proposed," Norm said carefully — from the southern tip of Texada to Homfray Channel was based on old names in their language and ancient usage. I traced the line on one map between Klahoose and Sliammon territory that cut Cortes in two, up to, and precisely including, the 1.5-kilometre-long wall in Gorge Harbour.

As Norm drove north past Hu'hjuusim, a small protected bay between Lund and Sliammon where rocks had been removed to create a better beach for clams, he agreed Flea Village had been a fort, but said that people were also "established" there more permanently and that the walled flat was indeed a clam garden. His look said "Well, of *course*."[3]

EPILOGUE

The people I had met or read about who had really lived on and from the land suggested more rock structure sites to examine and they strengthened my conviction that clams and clam gardens had played a vital, but minimally documented, role in indigenous economy. Susan Pielle's daughter Michelle Washington emailed from Sliammon with a list of Klahoose clam sites her brothers recalled: Prideaux Haven, Galley Bay, Von Donop Inlet, Rendezvous Islands, Whiterock Passage and the mouths of Teakerne Arm and Pendrell Sound. June Cameron exclaimed about the Mary Point clam flats on Cortes, where her family dug butters at 0.3-metre tides in the 1940s. These flats, she thinks, could now only be seen at a zero tide.

June asked if I remembered Kathrene Pinkerton's description in *Three's a Crew* of meeting Francine Hunt (Tsukwani), the Nakwaxda'xw second wife of Franz Boas's informant George Hunt, at Fort Rupert.[1] This fort was built at Beaver Harbour on Vancouver Island in 1849 for the Hudson's Bay Company, to exploit the nearby coal reserves. It became an important fur-trading centre, supplying goods and armaments that allowed for the Lekwiltok's southward incursion. Various members of the true Kwakiutl tribes (which had once included the Kweeha) settled permanently at Beaver Harbour, although middens and the petroglyphs below the fort site attest to a longer indigenous occupation. The Hudson's Bay factor, Robert Hunt, was married to a well-born Tlingit woman, and their daughter, Mrs. Spenser, and son, George (k'ixitasu), were sources for Franz Boas's publications on Kwakwaka'wakw culture. George became an accomplished Kwakwaka'wakw-style carver, dancer, ritual performer and translator. Hunt is now recognized as a significant indigenous anthropologist.

Kathrene wrote that when she and her husband Robert anchored their cruiser, *Triton*, at Fort Rupert in the early 1930s, George Hunt introduced her to Francine, "who was preparing winter clams for Indians who were still away fishing."

> Mrs Hunt was very large and very friendly and could not speak a word of English. She sat on the beach surrounded by clams. Hundreds were being smoked on racks. A washtub full was steamed and shucked.
>
> She motioned me to sit beside her while she wove clams on three long sticks. The two outer sticks were thrust through the bodies or pillows of the clams, while the necks were interlaced around the centre stick. One clam was strung on top of another. The plaiting was so beautifully regular that the finished product, a braid of clams two feet long and six inches wide, looked like an elaborate piece of knitting.
>
> I tried it but my plaited clams had great holes where I'd dropped clam stitches. We squatted there together, plaiting, smoking and stopping occasionally to eat a roasted clam. Talk was not necessary to establish a feeling of friendship and understanding.

As Kathrene "plaited clams all afternoon," the Pinkertons' daughter, Bobs, and Francine's nieces and nephews tended the low fires, and George told stories of his people.

Francine prodded George to show the Pinkertons the cookbook he was writing, which the missionaries disapproved of as something that would impede Native people's progress. George, Kathrene writes, "had visited the old women and written their native recipes."

In response to my enquiries about a picture of Francine Hunt, Dan Savard, photo archivist at the Royal BC Museum, recalled she had appeared digging clams in an Associated Screen News film, *Totem Land,* that is thought to have been made around 1927. The film concluded with scenes of George and Francine Hunt

Francine Hunt and George Hunt prepare clams, 1922.
BC ARCHIVES #PN-7287

at Fort Rupert, dancing and displaying traditional costumes and rattles. "Mrs. Hunt," identified as a skilled basket weaver and food provider, is filmed coming down to the sea edge of a white beach with her clam basket to gather a "shore dinner" with "clams as a first course." She vigorously stabs and pries her long digging stick into the very loose beach and scrapes sand away with a huge horse clam shell to bring up what appear to be butter clams. When she washes the clams, then stops and closely inspects one several times and, in the next scene, digs up and eats two cleaned rice root bulbs, then laughs so hard she falls out of the camera frame, it is clear she is engaged in skilled and familiar activities — digging root crops and clams from cultivated beds — and also clear why her companionship had so delighted Kathrene.

While I was viewing the film, Dan recalled a set of photographs taken in 1922 during an attempt by Pliny Earle Goddard, curator of ethnology at the American Museum of Natural History, to make a film. Dan drew from the files three close-up shots of Francine preparing clams (negative numbers PN-7285, PN-7286, and PN 7287), taken by Goddard. Two other stills (PN-869 and PN-6074) were taken by Dr. Charles Frederic Newcombe. In photo PN-7287, Francine and George sit on a shingle beach in front of a propped-up log next to a rough lean-to. George is whittling a cedar stick, and Francine has begun to lace large clams on a thin

Francine Hunt
opening a
cockle, 1922.
BC ARCHIVES
#PN-7286

stick. In front of Francine is a bentwood cedar box, and to her
left are two openwork clam baskets. Behind, on the log, is a line
of what appear to be shucked horse clams with their necks dan-
gling down. A considerable range of beach extends behind the
Hunts to trees in the background. In photo PN-7286, Francine has
lined up on the log the sticks braided with what, given their size,
might be those horse clams. She is opening what is clearly a large
cockle over a bucket behind the bentwood box. The two baskets
contain bivalves or shells. Barely visible upper left is a gas boat
beached near mooring poles and a cleated plank ramp. In photo
PN-7285, Francine seems to have moved slightly forward and is
squatting down, laying a braided set of clams on a cedar frame
over a low fire. There seems to be a fire in photo PN-869, too, in
which Francine stands with a stick in front of cedar mats behind
a veil of smoke or steam. This photo's higher viewpoint allows for
a glimpse of water in the background and a shell-surrounded islet
on the right with, perhaps, Cattle Islands behind. In photo PN-
6074, Francine seated in front of the shelter, box, and baskets as
George stands at the far right behind the camera and cinematog-
rapher, Goddard.

The bivalves identifiable in the photos are very large horse clams
(or geoducks?) and cockles. The Hunts' clothing indicates the pho-

tos were taken in the summer, and that is when horse clams were harvested and smoked. Butter clams were mainly procured in the winter. On our first trip upcoast in the *Adriatic Sea*, in 2000, we anchored in Beaver Harbour just north of Cattle Islands, which were surrounded by brilliant white beaches like those at Matilpi and Mound Island. I rowed ashore and, finding the sand decidedly "fluffy," easily dug up several horse clams for chowder using a large shell.

The photos and film scene were clearly taken to portray procurement and preparation of clams. George Hunt was in attendance both times and likely directed some scenes. However, while Boas and Hunt's extensive notes on customs, foods, and food preparation and storage in the *35th Annual Report of the Bureau of American Ethnology: 1913–1914* outline dozens of ways to prepare salmon and halibut; describe how to gather and correctly serve huckleberries, salmon milt, and salmonberry shoots; and include diagrams for constructing the correct basket in which to gather cinquefoil roots and other foods, they address clam harvesting and usage only four times. This is despite the fact that no one familiar with Northwest village life could fail to notice the massive consumption of clams where available.

Photographer Edward Curtis wrote: "Clams are an important tool to those who live in the vicinity of the clam bed; to others they are a comparative luxury obtained by barter."[2] A scene in his 1914 film *In the Land of the War Canoes* (some sections of which were directed by Hunt) shows a number of clam-digging women attacked by a canoe full of men. The traditionally garbed women run off, leaving their openwork clam baskets on the shore.[3] The film was partially shot on Deer Island, the old village and clam site Wazulis ("River on flat beach"), in Beaver Harbour. Deer Island was one Beaver Harbour site claimed in 1914 at the McKenna-McBride Commission by Kwakiutl Chief Owahagaleese and Charles Nowell for clams. They also claimed Aklanuzi (Cattle Islands), Kotsisae (Peel Island), Tsatsupathsen (one of the Masterman Islands), as well as Shell Island (Q!E'msex·La), closest to the fort, for clams. An old village site Yequilwa, on the mainland opposite Peel Island, was claimed for fishing and clams.[4] I would suggest that these sites, like those requested in the Broughtons and at New Church House, might be cultivated beds.

Since the Native people publicly exhibited a keen desire to preserve clam sites for shellfish harvesting, why was such a well-used
food, the related processing activities, and the structures that
made enhanced clam production possible, essentially absent from
Boas's published texts? The stories about Mink that Boas and Hunt
included in their publications suggest that low-tide levels could be
crucial to a group's well-being, but I can find no comment about
this relevance. These narratives, which we now acknowledge contain the history of a tribe's origin or establishment in a particular
location, were for a long time dismissed as "myth."

Still, it is hard to understand the information gap that arose
about clam gardens owned and cultivated in so many coastal
areas, and certainly within territory Boas recorded and George
Hunt is known to have contributed information about. In "Reconstructing Indigenous Resource Management, Reconstructing the
History of an Idea," the introduction to *Keeping it Living,* Nancy
Turner and Douglas Deur tackle the problem of Boas's lack of
published material on Northwest Coast plant cultivation. Their
thesis may apply to other cultivated foodstuffs. They find Boas's
public dismissal of Northwest Coast plant cultivation "enigmatic"
and cite cases in which he acknowledges data on plot location and
ownership. However, they argue that "Boas engaged in very little
field observation of these practices, and tended to underplay the
practices and testimonies of women or non-elite men, who were
the primary plant cultivators." They propose that it was Boas's
intent to undermine the prevailing orthodoxy of the time, which
regarded "hunter gatherer" societies to be incapable of the sophisti-
cated cultural development associated with agricultural societies.[5]
Boas presented the cultures of the Pacific Northwest as evidence
for his argument that hunter-gatherer societies, under favourable
conditions, could easily attain the sophistication of agricultural-
ists without having to cultivate crops. A side effect of the "Boa-
sian" view was that hunter gatherers were considered capable of
only the most tentative claims to land ownership. This proved of
great convenience to those settler interests, in the early years of
the province, that were intent on appropriation of aboriginal land
and resources.

A tendency developed among anthropologists and archeologists to overlook evidence that Boas himself found little use for.

As a result, evidence of active management and manipulation of natural resources wasn't conserved in "the literature," and that fact, combined with the lack of fieldwork that might have uncovered the rock-walled terraces, contributed to the professional skepticism among archeologists when John Harper and I independently presented evidence that people had constructed terraces specifically to enhance bivalve cultivation.

Perhaps it took a woman like Kathrene, a writer who cooked food she foraged as her family boated upcoast, to admire the skill involved in clam processing and to consider it important to publish that information.

Now that the existence of clam garden cultivation is being accepted, we cannot ignore the importance of ancient clam beds and other traditional food resources to the contemporary economy of Native communities. The sinking of the *Queen of the North* ferry on Gil Island at the southern end of Grenville Channel on March 22, 2006, was not simply a maritime disaster, with regrettable loss of life and a truncation of transportation for northern communities. The sad irony is that the Native people of nearby Hartley Bay, who sped to the rescue of passengers and crew, were entering the season in which herring roe is gathered on kelp, as was once done at Sliammon village and as is still done in Bella Bella. The people of Hartley Bay are now concerned that this harvest, and that of the incredibly productive clam beds nearby, which remain (as at Gilford Island) vital elements of their mixed economy, will be contaminated by the vessel's leaking fuel.[6]

The clam gardens were and are a coastal treasure. Unique *living* artifacts, they are still usable sources of food and exchange items for the local population. This primary mariculture technology of the Northwest Pacific should be protected for the descendants of those who created it.

APPENDIX

One of the four notes referring to bivalves in Boas and Hunt's *35th Annual Report of the Bureau of American Ethnology: 1913–1914* details how a woman prepares clams for her husband to use to catch flounders.

> When it is a fine day, the wife of the man gets ready in the morning to get clams and cockles for bait. When she has many she goes home to her house. As soon as she arrives on the beach of her house, she takes a piece of a broken shell of a horse clam and cuts open the small clams to take off the shells ... she throws these into the water and puts the edible parts into a basket.

The report also describes the use of broken-open clams as bait in a perch trap and includes directions for steaming devilfish with clams. Another recipe suggests opened clams be soaked in a small amount of water, squeezed into a container with oolichan oil, boiled with hot rocks, and seaweed added.

Despite testy claims by Mink's mother that barnacles were useless, the text suggests roasting them on the beach by lighting a fire on the rocks they're attached to.

CLAM BAKE

In Bouchard and Kennedy's 1970s notes, Rose Mitchell describes a process shown in a Cordova Bay photograph: "If butter clams, little necks or horse clams are to be cooked, a pit is dug as for cooking fern roots and lined with hot rocks lifted from a fire. These were covered with cedar bark and clams put in. The pit was covered by a tule mat and steamed for half an hour."

She says if clams were to be preserved, they were threaded on ironwood sticks (*xwup'emin*) poked through the body of the clam and the pallial muscles were twisted around the body. In the last step, the

siphon, *yaymay*, was also skewered by the stick. "The process of threading the clams is called *xwup'uwulhkwu*."[1]

Rose says the sticks were leaned against a horizontal pole facing the
fire and turned half way for half an hour. If needed for winter, they were
smoked on the sticks, which were bent over a pole in the roof of the
smoke house. The clams were removed from the sticks, a cedar plank
was laid over them, and someone walked on the plank to squeeze out
the excess moisture. The clams were then threaded on red cedar bark,
tied in a loop, and hung to dry further.

Later they could be soaked and dipped in seal or oolichan oil, and
during one visit to Flora Dawson in GwaYi village in Kingcome Inlet,
dried smoked clams dipped in mighty strong-tasting oolichan oil formed
an unforgettable appetizer to our lunch.

*Indian clam
bake, Cordova
Bay, c. 1900.*
BC ARCHIVES
#G-04230

BILLY PROCTOR ON BUTTER CLAMS

"We take the whole siphon off and Yvonne always removes the gills.
Most of the time if you do this they will be fine as 90 percent of the
poison is in the siphon and gills. We only eat clams when there is an R
in the month."

Clam chowder: "About eight to ten butter clams, one onion, one or
two spuds, two carrots. We put everything through a food chopper. Add
salt and pepper and a bit of dried parsley." (I strongly suggest adding
clam nectar, water, or milk.)

Clam fritters: "Mix two cups of ground butter clams, 1/2 cup flour, 1/2
cup canned milk, one onion, one teaspoon Worcestershire sauce or soy

sauce. Salt and pepper to taste. Heat pan and oil and cook until fritters bounce off bottom of pan. Turn to brown and drain."

Fried clams: "We don't use the stomach, we use the frills and butt ends and fry them in butter. You can use the whole clam. Slice the stomach open and lay it gut side down. This is good with small butter clams."

AMELIA'S CAT HOUSE CLAMS

Split butter clam shells and bodies with a knife, drain raw, and dip the open side into batter. Fry half a clam, batter-side down, on a griddle.

JUDY'S BUTTER CLAM CHOWDER

Procure clams by digging, buying frozen clam meat from Mac's Oysters, or opening St. Jean's canned clams and nectar. Open live clams raw, save nectar, and remove siphons.

Sauté three slices of chopped gammon bacon and drain. Turn one cup chopped onion, three or four cubed carrots, and two cubed large potatoes and turn in gammon fat. Pour over two cups of clam nectar and a cup of water. Add one cup chopped celery halfway through. Cook until vegetables soften. Lightly mash about 1/3 of vegetables, leaving lots of lumps. Potato starch will thicken chowder. Add chunked clam bodies to pot. Bring gently to a boil, turn down heat, and add one cup milk. Heat but do not boil. Ladle into bowls, slide one tablespoon of cream across top, and sprinkle with finely chopped fresh parsley. Pepper to taste. Do not on any account add salt. You may add 1/2 pound snapper chunks during the last heating.

To use horse clams, blanch the neck, remove the black covering, and chop finely.

BC FERRIES CHOWDER

The current, and overly cornstarched, BC Ferries clam chowder is made with a butter clam base and "Asian" (Manila?) clams. I fear the latter may be canned. The butters are processed by Global Gourmet from those frozen in the shell by Mac's Oysters.

WILLIAM SCOW BARBEQUED CLAMS

"You know we barbeque clams, and it's delicious. You lay the clams on top of the fire . . . in the shell. The nectar is embedded right into the body of the clam."

ACKNOWLEDGMENTS AND NOTES

The archeological resistance to recognizing the Quadra Island clam gardens, which the late Elizabeth Harry (Keekus) introduced me to in 1993, was resolved through the persistence of Dr. John Harper. John's determination to gain official recognition for similar Broughton Archipelago clam terraces as evidence of Native mariculture was the work of a scientist able to see beyond the roadblocks of received opinion. His acceptance of Chief Adam Dick's Kwakwalla term lo xwi we referring to the rock walls supporting the gardens, and Billy Proctor's sharing of current use data, were the vital keys to solving the clam garden puzzle. I am grateful for permission to reproduce John's aerial photos.

Calvin Harry of the Homalco band arranged my first meeting with Keekus, and Randy Bouchard and Dorothy Kennedy's conversations with Keekus and her parents, Chief William Mitchell and Rose Mitchell, in Sliammon Life, Sliammon Lands and in documents they made available to me in the 1990s were pivotal to my understanding of Mainland Comox clam technology. Michelle Washington shared photos and information from the Mitchell and Harry families. Dr. Don Mitchell, Mary Morris, Dr. Nancy Turner, Norm Gibbons, Dan Savard, Don Pepper, Linda Hogarth and June Cameron added depth to my research. Neil Bourne elucidated the life cycle of the butter clam, and Judge Alfred Scow and Alvin (Bear) Scow offered William Scow's reminiscences of his clam packing days. Norm Gallagher provided an eye-opening tour of Sliammon rock-walled food recruitment structures. Site report information is from the Heritage Conservation Department of the BC Ministry of Tourism, Sport and the Arts.

I very much appreciate the support of Terry Glavin and of publisher Rolf Maurer, and the intelligent editing skills of Audrey McClellan. I'm deeply indebted to my husband, Robert (Bobo) Fraser, and to our skookum speedboat Tetacus, named, in 1989, after the Chief who provided Captain Cayetano Valdes with smoked clams in 1792.

PROLOGUE

1. Bill Proctor and Yvonne Maximchuck, Full Moon, Flood Tide: Bill Proctor's Raincoast (Madeira Park, BC: Harbour Publishing, 2003).

2. The place name cited may also be Cikwalis, meaning "clam-steaming-on-beach-place." Franz Boas, Indian Myth and Legends from the North Pacific Coast of America, ed. and annotated by Randy Bouchard and Dorothy Kennedy, trans. Dietrich Bertz (Vancouver: Talonbooks, 2002). Originally published as Indianishe Sagen von der Nord-Pacifishen Kuste Amerikas (1895). Boas recorded "Children of the Dog" story from the Bella Bella and the Kwakwalla-speaking Lekwiltok with a Sliammon variant. Dog

Rib storyteller Richard Van Camp relates a version about the origin of his people, and he found contemporary Salish people at Musqueam tell the same tale.

1. KEEKUS

1. Judith Williams, *High Slack*, University of British Columbia Museum of Anthropology, 1994. Judith Williams, *High Slack: Waddington's Gold Road and the Bute Inlet Massacre of 1864* (Vancouver: New Star Books, 1996).

2. Randy Bouchard and Dorothy Kennedy, *Sliammon Life, Sliammon Lands* (Vancouver: Talon Books, 1983).

2. RAVEN WALK

1. June Cameron, *Destination Cortez Island: A Sailor's Life Along the B.C. Coast* (Surrey, BC: Heritage House, 1999).

2. Nancy A. Greene, "A New Angle On Northwest Coast Fish Trap Technologies: Gis Total Mapping Of Intertidal Wood-Stake Features At Comox Harbour, B.C." (paper presented at the Canadian Archaeological Association Annual Conference in Nanaimo, 2005).

3. Rick M. Harbo, *Shells and Shellfish of the Pacific Northwest: A Field Guide* (Madeira Park, BC: Harbour Publishing, 2001).

4. Kenneth M. Ames and Herbert D.G. Maschner, *Peoples of the Northwest Coast: Their Archaeology and Prehistory* (London: Thames and Hudson, 1999).

5. Judith Williams, *Two Wolves at the Dawn of Time: Kingcome Inlet Pictographs 1893–1989* (Vancouver: New Star Books, 2002).

6. Proctor and Maximchuk, *Full Moon, Flood Tide: Bill Proctor's Raincoast.*

7. Arranged from Franz Boas and George Hunt, *Kwakiutl Texts*, vol. 10, *The Jesup North Pacific Expedition* (New York: G.E. Stechert and Co., 1906).

3. BEST CLAMS ON THE COAST

1. Rick M. Harbo, *Shells and Shellfish of the Pacific Northwest: A Field Guide* (Madeira Park, BC: Harbour Publishing, 2001).

2. Renée Hetherington, J. Vaughn Barrie, Roger MacLeod and Michael Wilson, "Quest for the Lost Land," *Geotimes*, February 2004.

3. D.B. Quale and N. Bourne, *The Clam Fisheries of British Columbia*, Bulletin 179, Fisheries Research Board of Canada, Biological Station, Nanaimo, BC (Ottawa: Information Canada, 1972).

4. Boas, *Indian Myth and Legends from the North Pacific Coast of America.*

5. William Scow tape transcripts courtesy of Judge Alfred Scow and Alvin Scow.

4. OPEN THAT ENVELOPE, PLEASE!

1. Quotes from Dr. John Harper are drawn from a Stephen Hume article in the *Vancouver Sun* on October 25, 2003, and from Terry Glavin's *Georgia Straight* column of October 23, 2003, from cited reports, and from personal communications or conversations.

2. Hume, *Vancouver Sun.*

3. Story from James King of Wakeman Sound, included in Audrey Hawthorn, *Kwakiutl Art* (Vancouver: Douglas and McIntyre, 1988).

4. Bernhard J. Stern, *The Lummi Indians of Northwest Washington* (New York: Columbia University Press, 1934).

5. Douglas Deur, "A Domesticated Landscape: Native American Plant Cultivation on the Northwest Coast of North America" (PhD dissertation, Dept. of Geography and Anthropology, Louisiana State University, 2000).

6. *Ancient Sea Gardens: Mystery of the Pacific Northwest*, DVD, directed by Aaron Szimanski, produced by D. J. Woods Productions (Toronto: Aquaculture Pictures, 2005).

7. Hume, *Vancouver Sun.*

8. Verbatim transcript of an excerpt of a May 1974 tape-recorded interview of Rose and Bill Mitchell and Elizabeth Harry at Sliammon, by Dorothy Kennedy and Randy Bouchard, BC Indian Language Project, Victoria.

5. WHO, WHEN, WHERE, AND WHY?

1. Robert Galois, *Kwakwaka'wakw Settlements, 1775–1920: A Geographical Analysis and Gazetteer* (Vancouver: UBC Press, 1994).

2. Bouchard and Kennedy, *Sliammon Life, Sliammon Lands.*

3. Galois, *Kwakwaka'wakw Settlements.*

4. Randy Bouchard and Dorothy Kennedy,

"Northern Coast Salish" in *Northwest Coast*, ed. Wayne Suttles, vol. 7, *Handbook of the North American Indians* (Washington, DC: Smithsonian Institution, 1990).

5. Martin Fernandez de Navarrete, *A Spanish Voyage To Vancouver and the Northwest Coast of America*, trans. Cecil Jane (London: The Argonaut Press, 1930).

6. Galois, *Kwakwaka'wakw Settlements*.

7. Ames and Maschner, *Peoples of the Northwest Coast: Their Archaeology and Prehistory*.

6. OTHER DIRECTIONS

1. Randy Bouchard and Dorothy Kennedy, "Utilization of Fishes, Beach Foods and Marine Animals by the Tl'uhus Indian People of British Columbia" (preliminary draft of unpublished manuscript).

2. Ibid.

3. Ibid.

4. The *tabla* is described in greater detail in Williams, *High Slack: Waddington's Gold Road and the Bute Inlet Massacre of 1864*.

5. Homer Barnett, *The Coast Salish of B.C.* (Eugene: University of Oregon Press, 1955).

7. ABODE OF SUPERNATURAL BEINGS

1. Franz Boas and George Hunt, *35th Annual Report of the Bureau of American Ethnology: 1913–1914* (Washington: US Government, 1921).

2. George Vancouver, *A Voyage of Discovery to the North Pacific Ocean and Round the World 1791–1795*, Volume 2 (London: The Hakluyt Society, 1984).

8. GATHERING AT THE END OF THE ROAD

1. Adapted from a tale told by "Eldrbarry."

9. 'WE CAN'T COUNT THE YEARS ...'

1. The April 2006 *Hamatsa Treaty Society Newsletter* states that fish traps in Comox Harbour are at least 1,800 years old and are related to clam garden technology in Blenkin-sop Bay south of Port Neville.

2. John Harper *et al.*, "Clam Gardens of British Columbia" (paper presented at the Canadian Archaeological Association Annual Conference in Nanaimo, 2005).

3. Norm Gallager died suddenly in October 2005. I deeply appreciate his effort, like Keekus's, to pass information about stone structures on to someone who would write it down.

EPILOGUE

1. Kathrene Pinkerton, *Three's a Crew* (New York: Carrick and Evans, 1940). The Pinkertons travelled the West Coast in the 1930s for seven years.

2. Edward Curtis, *The North American Indian*, vol. 9, ed. Frederick Webb Hodge (New York: Johnson Reprint, 1970. Reprint of the 1907-1930 edition).

3. In *In the Land of the War Canoes* women are outfitted in the cedar-bark skirts, blankets, and hats that Nakoakloh is shown wearing on the front cover. Curtis costumed his actors in clothing that, although accurate, was not still worn in 1914. However, the openwork clam baskets were used by Francine Hunt in the 1920s.

4. Robert Galois, *Kwakwaka'wakw Settlements, 1775–1920: A Geographical Analysis and Gazetteer* (Vancouver: UBC Press, 1994).

5. Douglas Deur and Nancy J. Turner, eds., *Keeping it Living: Traditions of Plant Use and Cultivation on the Northwest Coast of North America* (Vancouver/Seattle: UBC Press/University of Washington Press, 2005).

6. Hereditary Chiefs Albert Clifton and Ernie Hill Jr., *Vancouver Sun*, Thursday, March 30, 2006.

APPENDIX

1. Bouchard and Kennedy, "Utilization of Fishes, Beach Foods and Marine Animals."

2. Boas and Hunt, *35th Annual Report of the Bureau of American Ethnology: 1913–1914*.

INDEX

Abbott, Donald N. 37, 75-76
Ames, Kenneth 60-61
Ancient Sea Gardens (film) 49, 92, 100
anthropologists 48, 118-19. *See also* Boas, Franz
archeologists: focus on salmon 61; clam gardens 11, 20, 25, 27, 37, 46, 52, 65, 75, 95, 118-19; limits on vision 92, 93
Assu, Harry 59, 95
Barnes, Joe 70
Barnett, Homer 72-73
Barrie, J. Vaughn 32
Beauchamp, Erica 74-76
Beaver Harbour 113, 117
Boas, Franz 26, 113: clams 48, 117, 118; hunter-gatherer theory 118; Lekwiltok 57-58
Bonwick Island 52
Bouchard, Randy 47-50, 74
Bourne, Neil 34-37, 40
Broughton Archipelago 39, 43, 88: clam gardens 10-11, 44, 45, 83-84, 86-87, 89-90; historic population 87; map 42; red tide 46. *See also specific locations*
butter clams 29, 31, 39, 60, 61: commercial market 33, 37-38, 40, 45; growing conditions 33-37, 51, 76; red tide 22-23
Cameron, June 23, 113
canoe slides 29, 36, 65, 96
Cesaholis (Chief) 87
Chickite, Ollie 73
clam gardens 6, 11-12: associated

with women 48, 93, 115-19; builders 53 (*See also specific groups*); construction of 10, 36, 49, 50, 65, 87; dating of 32, 100; description 9-10, 29, 44-45, 49, 52 (*See also specific sites*); ideal conditions for 17, 25, 35-37, 63, 95, 104-5, 118; locations 9, 71, 100, 102, 113; overlooked references 11, 20, 28, 40, 46-48, 49, 118-19 (*See also* archeologists); ownership 29, 33, 36, 49, 90; part of food complex 21, 59, 84, 86, 107, 110-11; population density related to 59-60; productivity 10, 31, 32-33, 36, 47, 77, 83, 86; untended 77, 86, 88
clams 48, 117, 119. *See also specific types*
Coast Salish 55-57, 59, 96, 111-12. *See also* Mainland Comox, Island Comox
Codville Lagoon 101-2
Cortes Island 103-5, 112
Curtis, Edward 30, 117
Deur, Douglas 49, 118
devilfish. *See* octopus
Dewar, Anne 103, 105
Dick, Adam 47-48, 49, 93
"Dog Skins" song 13, 47-48, 51
Edith Island 62, 67
First Nations: alter landscape 27-28, 76, 87, 102; and clams 36, 38-39 (*See also* clam gardens); complex presence in landscape 74, 79, 102, 103;

diet 28, 29, 31, 33, 60-61, 102; economy 46, 48, 61, 100; European views of 11-12, 27-28, 51, 61, 118-19; historic population 51, 59-60; "hunter gatherers" 12, 27-28, 118; mariculture 11-12, 102; ownership of food resources 32, 49, 60-61, 89, 90, 95, 118 (*See also* Quadra Island); rock art 78-80 (*See also* pictographs, petroglyphs)
fish traps 25-26, 68, 107
Fladmark, K.R. 60-61
Flea Village 106, 108-9, 112
Francis, Roy 70
Franke, Walter 18, 65
Gallagher, Norm 64, 109-12
Galois, Robert 56-57, 59, 95
geoduck clam 40
Gibbons, Norm 104-5, 111
Gilford Island 28-29, 39, 82
Glavin, Terry 15, 49
Glendale, William 58
Goddard, Pliny Earle 115
Gorge Harbour 103-5, 112
Grace Harbour 63-67
Greene, Nancy A. 25-26
Grief Point 110-11
Gunther, Erna 71
Haggarty, James 45, 46
Halliday, Alan 28
Hanson, Helen 70
Hanson, Larry 70
Hanuse, Ken 73
Harbo, Rick 26
Hare Point 65
Harper, John 9, 10, 15: in

Broughton 43-47, 49, 82-83; at Kanish Bay 92, 95
Harry, Calvin 20, 23
Harry, Elizabeth. *See* Keekus
Henderson, James 57
Hetheringon, Renee 32
Hogarth, Linda 63, 94
Homalco. *See* Mainland Comox
Homfray, Robert 15-16, 73, 108
horse clams 31, 34
Humchitt, Carl 100, 102
Hunt, Francine 113-17
Hunt, George 113-17, 118
In the Land of the War Canoes 117
Inglis, Joy 27, 79, 96
Island Comox 53, 54-56: historic territories 54-56, 57, 58, 76; and Mainland Comox 72-73, 111
Julian (Chief) 64, 73
Kanish Bay 24, 59, 63, 91-92, 94, 95-97: map 14
Kearns, Lionel 51-52
Keekus 10, 16, 43, 50, 97
Kennedy, Dorothy 47, 50
Klahoose. *See* Mainland Comox
Kukwapa 87
Kwakwaka'wakw people 53-54, 56-57: in Kanish Bay 95
Kwiksootainuk people 46, 53, 54, 82
Lalakinnis (Chief) 58
Lekwiltok people 54, 56-58, 59, 76, 96
littleneck clams 31, 33, 40
lo xwi we 48, 110
Louie, Danny 70
MacLeod, Roger 32
Mainland Comox people 16, 53, 54-56: clam gardens 63, 65-67, 70, 71-74; historic territory 54-56, 57, 59, 64, 70-71, 105; and Island Comox 72-73; unity of three groups 72-73, 111
Malaspina Inlet 63-70, 109
Mamalilikulla people 54, 89-90
Manila clams 33, 40
Martin, Mungo 59
Maschner, Herbert 60-61
Maximchuk, Yvonne 29, 84
McKenna-McBride Royal Commission 53-54, 117

Menzies, Archibald 55, 108
middens 31, 32, 60
Mink stories 5, 30, 48, 81, 82, 118
Mitchell, Don 37, 54, 87, 91, 92, 94-96
Mitchell, Joe 74
Mitchell, Joseph 16
Mitchell, Rose 16, 43, 50, 67, 70
Mitchell, William 16, 50
molluscs, on West Coast 31-32, 49. *See also specific species*
Monday Anchorage 81, 84, 86
Moon, Peter 47
Morris, Mary 45, 47, 49, 82-83, 92, 93
Mound Island. *See* Tsaite
Mountain, Harry 54, 89
mussels 31, 33
myth 51, 118
Namgis First Nation 52
Nowell, Charles 117
octopus 84, 85
Owahagaleese (Chief) 117
oysters 40, 104-5, 111
Pepper, Don 37-38
petroglyphs 26, 78-80
pictographs 69, 72, 77, 78-80, 82, 91, 101-2
Pielle, Susan 16, 59, 112, 113
Pinkerton, Kathrene 113-14, 119
Portage Cove 62, 69-70, 108
Powell River 110-11
Prideaux Haven 106-9
Proctor, Billy 9, 28, 29, 47, 82, 83, 86, 88
Proctor, Yvonne 83
Quadra Island 26: Native control of 54-55, 57, 58. *See also* Kanish Bay, Waiatt Bay
Quale, D.B. 34
Raven and the First Men 98
Recalma-Clutesi, Kim 47, 49, 93
red tide 22-23, 46, 83
Ricketts, Ed 86
Ripple Rock 55
Robinson, Kevin 52
salmon: access to 60, 79, 90; seen as economic engine 48, 61. *See also* fish traps
Savard, Dan 114-15
Saxidomus giganteus. See butter clam
Scow, Johnny 53-54, 55, 89

Scow, William 38-39, 86
Sewid, Tom 36
Sewid-Smith, Daisy 47, 49
Shoal Harbour 28
Simonson, Bjorn 75
Sliammon Life, Sliammon Lands 16
Sliammon. *See* Mainland Comox
smallpox 57
Smith, Peter 57
Snout Point 70, 71-73
Sproat, G.M. 58
Stern, Bernhard J. 49
Stewart, Hilary 26, 27, 79
T'eshusm 108, 109-10
t'i`mi`q 110
Tatapowis 17, 58-59
Tetacus (Chief) 58, 60
Theodosia Inlet 62, 68-69, 109
Toba Inlet 70, 71
Tsaite 54, 58
Turner, Nancy 47, 92-93, 96, 118
Valdes, Cayetano 58, 60
Vancouver, George 22, 55, 89
Village Island 89-90
Waiatt Bay (Ga y at) 59, 74-77: as clam garden location 16-22, 23-27, 36-37; historic ownership of 54, 78, 111-12 (*See also* Island Comox people, Lekwiltok); map 14, 74; photo 79
Wamish, Tom 47
Washington, Michelle 113
Williams, Judith: books 15-16, 28; in Broughton 82-89; and John Harper 15, 43, 49-52; at Kanish Bay 91-97; and Keekus 10, 12, 16; list of clam gardens 71; other sites 63-72, 100-12; pictographs 78-80; at Waiatt Bay 16-25, 27, 74-78
Williams, June 112
Willie, Billie Sandy 47
Wilson, Michael 32
women: and anthropologists 48, 93, 114, 118; and clams 13, 30, 48, 49, 61, 85, 93, 102, 115-19; informants 15, 43, 75
Woodward, Curly 110
wuxwuthin 43, 50, 65, 110
Yay K Wum (Chief) 15-16, 73

NEW STAR BOOKS LTD.

107 - 3477 Commercial Street, Vancouver, BC V5N 4E8   CANADA
1574 Gulf Road, No. 1517, Point Roberts, WA 9828   USA
www.NewStarBooks.com   info@NewStarBooks.com

TRANSMONTANUS is edited by Terry Glavin. Editorial correspondence
should be sent to 3813 Hobbs Street, Victoria, BC   V8P 5C8
terry.glavin@gmail.com

Edited by Audrey McClellan
Cover by Mutasis.com
Photos by Judith Williams unless otherwise indicated
Maps by Eric Leinberger
Typesetting by New Star Books
Printed & bound in Canada by Friesens Printing
First printing, November 2006. Reprinted 2008
Printed on 100% post-consumer recycled paper

The publisher acknowledges the financial support of the Government
of Canada through the Canada Council and the Department of Canadian Heritage Book Publishing Industry Development Program, and
of the Province of British Columbia through the British Columbia Arts
Council and the Book Publishing Tax Credit.

LIBRARY AND ARCHIVES CANADA CATALOGUING IN PUBLICATION

Williams, Judith, 1940–
    Clam gardens: Aboriginal mariculture on Canada's west coast /
Judith Williams.

Includes index.
ISBN 1-55420-023-7
    1. Clam culture — British Columbia — Broughton Island — His-
tory.   2. Clam culture — British Columbia — Cortes Island — History.   3. Indians of North America — Fishing — British Columbia
— Broughton Island.   4. Indians of North America — Fishing — British Columbia — Cortes Island.   I. Title.
E78.B9W54 2006   639'.44'0899707111   C2006-900570-2